INTRODUCING
ISSUES WITH
OPPOSING
VIEWPOINTS®

Food Safety

Noël Merino, *Book Editor*

GREENHAVEN PRESS
A part of Gale, Cengage Learning

GALE
CENGAGE Learning™

Detroit • New York • San Francisco • New Haven, Conn • Waterville, Maine • London

Elizabeth Des Chenes, *Managing Editor*

© 2012 Greenhaven Press, a part of Gale, Cengage Learning

Gale and Greenhaven Press are registered trademarks used herein under license.

For more information, contact:
Greenhaven Press
27500 Drake Rd.
Farmington Hills, MI 48331-3535
Or you can visit our Internet site at gale.cengage.com

For product information and technology assistance, contact us at

Gale Customer Support, 1-800-877-4253
For permission to use material from this text or product, submit all requests online at
www.cengage.com/permissions

Further permissions questions can be e-mailed to permissionrequest@cengage.com

Articles in Greenhaven Press anthologies are often edited for length to meet page requirements. In addition, original titles of these works are changed to clearly present the main thesis and to explicitly indicate the author's opinion. Every effort is made to ensure that Greenhaven Press accurately reflects the original intent of the authors. Every effort has been made to trace the owners of copyrighted material.

Cover image © IMAGEMORE Co., Ltd./Alamy

LIBRARY OF CONGRESS CATALOGING-IN-PUBLICATION DATA

Food safety / Noël Merino, book editor.
    p. cm. -- (Introducing issues with opposing viewpoints)
  Summary: "Food Safety: Does the Current US System Ensure Food Safety?; Are New Food Technologies Safe?; Are Certain Foods Unsafe to Eat?"-- Provided by publisher.
  Includes bibliographical references and index.
  ISBN 978-0-7377-5678-4 (hardback)
  1. Food adulteration and inspection--United States. 2. Food industry and trade--United States--Safety measures. 3. Food--Biotechnology--Safety measures. I. Merino, Noël.
  TX531.F56773 2011
  363.19'20973--dc23
                                                                    2011014081

Printed in the United States of America
1 2 3 4 5 6 7 15 14 13 12 11

Contents

Foreword

I ndulging in a wide spectrum of ideas, beliefs, and perspectives is a critical cornerstone of democracy. After all, it is often debates over differences of opinion, such as whether to legalize abortion, how to treat prisoners, or when to enact the death penalty, that shape our society and drive it forward. Such diversity of thought is frequently regarded as the hallmark of a healthy and civilized culture. As the Reverend Clifford Schutjer of the First Congregational Church in Mansfield, Ohio, declared in a 2001 sermon, "Surrounding oneself with only like-minded people, restricting what we listen to or read only to what we find agreeable is irresponsible. Refusing to entertain doubts once we make up our minds is a subtle but deadly form of arrogance." With this advice in mind, Introducing Issues with Opposing Viewpoints books aim to open readers' minds to the critically divergent views that comprise our world's most important debates.

Introducing Issues with Opposing Viewpoints simplifies for students the enormous and often overwhelming mass of material now available via print and electronic media. Collected in every volume is an array of opinions that captures the essence of a particular controversy or topic. Introducing Issues with Opposing Viewpoints books embody the spirit of nineteenth-century journalist Charles A. Dana's axiom: "Fight for your opinions, but do not believe that they contain the whole truth, or the only truth." Absorbing such contrasting opinions teaches students to analyze the strength of an argument and compare it to its opposition. From this process readers can inform and strengthen their own opinions, or be exposed to new information that will change their minds. Introducing Issues with Opposing Viewpoints is a mosaic of different voices. The authors are statesmen, pundits, academics, journalists, corporations, and ordinary people who have felt compelled to share their experiences and ideas in a public forum. Their words have been collected from newspapers, journals, books, speeches, interviews, and the Internet, the fastest growing body of opinionated material in the world.

Introducing Issues with Opposing Viewpoints shares many of the well-known features of its critically acclaimed parent series, Opposing Viewpoints. The articles are presented in a pro/con format, allowing readers to absorb divergent perspectives side by side. Active reading questions preface each viewpoint, requiring the student to approach the material thoughtfully and carefully. Useful charts, graphs, and cartoons supplement each article. A thorough introduction provides readers with crucial background on an issue. An annotated bibliography points the reader toward articles, books, and websites that contain additional information on the topic. An appendix of organizations to contact contains a wide variety of charities, nonprofit organizations, political groups, and private enterprises that each hold a position on the issue at hand. Finally, a comprehensive index allows readers to locate content quickly and efficiently.

Introducing Issues with Opposing Viewpoints is also significantly different from Opposing Viewpoints. As the series title implies, its presentation will help introduce students to the concept of opposing viewpoints and learn to use this material to aid in critical writing and debate. The series' four-color, accessible format makes the books attractive and inviting to readers of all levels. In addition, each viewpoint has been carefully edited to maximize a reader's understanding of the content. Short but thorough viewpoints capture the essence of an argument. A substantial, thought-provoking essay question placed at the end of each viewpoint asks the student to further investigate the issues raised in the viewpoint, compare and contrast two authors' arguments, or consider how one might go about forming an opinion on the topic at hand. Each viewpoint contains sidebars that include at-a-glance information and handy statistics. A Facts About section located in the back of the book further supplies students with relevant facts and figures.

Following in the tradition of the Opposing Viewpoints series, Greenhaven Press continues to provide readers with invaluable exposure to the controversial issues that shape our world. As John Stuart Mill once wrote: "The only way in which a human being can make some approach to knowing the whole of a subject is by hearing what can be said about it by persons of every variety of opinion and studying all modes in which it can be looked at by every character of mind. No wise man ever acquired his wisdom in any mode but this." It is to this principle that Introducing Issues with Opposing Viewpoints books are dedicated.

Introduction

"There are certain things only a government can do. And one of those things is ensuring that the foods we eat are safe and do not cause us harm."

—President Barack Obama

In 1862 President Abraham Lincoln founded the US Department of Agriculture (USDA) and the Bureau of Chemistry. The USDA, through the Bureau of Animal Industry, regulated the meat-processing industry beginning in the late nineteenth century. In 1906 Congress passed the Pure Food and Drug Act, to be enforced by the Bureau of Chemistry, which prohibited the interstate commerce of misbranded and adulterated food, drinks, and drugs. That same year it also passed the Meat Inspection Act, enforced by the Bureau of Animal Industry. In 1931 the US Food and Drug Administration (FDA) was formally created—an offshoot of the original Bureau of Chemistry. In 1977 the Food Safety and Quality Service was established within the USDA, and in 1981 it was renamed the Food Safety and Inspection Service (FSIS). To this day the FSIS and the FDA are responsible for the nation's food safety. The FSIS focuses on the safety of meat, poultry, and egg products, whereas the FDA is responsible for the safety of all other food products. One of the most historic pieces of food safety legislation to pass in many decades is the FDA Food Safety Modernization Act, signed by President Barack Obama on January 4, 2011.

The Food Safety Modernization Act aims to prevent food-borne illness and respond to outbreaks better by granting more authority to the FDA. The Center for Science in the Public Interest notes, "Until now, the Food and Drug Administration has been charged with picking up the pieces after people get sick."[1] The Food Safety Modernization Act focuses on several key food safety issues: increasing food safety inspections at domestic and foreign manufacturing and processing facilities, requiring these facilities to take measures to prevent contamination, identifying foods at high risk for food-borne illness outbreaks, and developing an electronic tracking system that will follow food from the farm to consumption.

There is much hope that the new law will increase food safety. A spokesperson for the White House claims, "This law represents a sea change for food safety in America, bringing a new focus on prevention, and I expect that in the coming years it will have a dramatic and positive effect on the safety of the food supply."[2] The food safety director of the Center for Science in the Public Interest, an organization that campaigned for passage of the law, says, "This is a historic victory for consumers, who can now look forward to a future of safer food."[3] The executive director of the center goes even further, claiming, "Soon parents should be able to shop without worrying that the spinach, tomatoes, peanut butter, or eggs in their cart are going to cause illness and misery."[4]

Others are not convinced that the Food Safety Modernization Act will have much of an impact on food safety. Some, such as consultant Len Steiner, warn about the danger of the legislation lulling people into a false sense of security about food safety: "The fact is, 100 years from now dangerous varieties of E. coli will still be present in food no matter how many laws our politicians in Washington, DC, pass or how many technologies the food industry brings to bear on the pathogen problem."[5] Others, such as food writer Anastacia Marx de Salcedo, claim that the bill does not address the biggest source of food-borne illness: "More than 90 percent of foodborne illnesses occur within a vast, loosely organized network of rogue microbe breeders: restaurants! (about half of all outbreaks) and a motley assortment of workplaces, banquet facilities, caterers, churches, nursing homes, schools and others."[6]

For farmers the review is mixed. The National Farmers Union applauded the passage of the legislation. The law does exempt farmers who have less than five hundred thousand dollars in sales annually. However, some farmers are worried that the increased regulation for farmers who have sales greater than this amount may put them out of business. Reporter Mike Adams explains: "Small farmers who find even a little bit of success selling food (because selling $500,000 worth of food is still a very small scale operation, and the actual profit on that might only be $50,000 for a full year of work) are about to find themselves punished for being successful."[7]

Although the Food Safety Modernization Act gives the FDA greater power to work to increase food safety, it does not grant the FDA any additional money to do so. The Congressional Budget Office estimates that the Food Safety Modernization Act will cost about $1.4 billion in its first five years, including the cost of hiring two thousand additional food inspectors. The passage of the act now presents the FDA with the challenge of securing the funding required to implement and enforce the new system. The director of the Pew Health Group, who vowed to lobby Congress to increase funding for the FDA, stated: "The costs of not implementing the law are staggering, and it would be money well spent."[8] The FDA will need funding to be able to exercise the new powers granted to it and implement the changes in the law.

Food safety is an issue that touches everyone. The development of the federal agencies in charge of ensuring the safety of the US food supply was an outgrowth of that concern over a century ago. Today the country still wrestles with how best to utilize these agencies to ensure safe food. There is much disagreement about how much power these federal agencies should have, not to mention disagreement about whether or not there is a food safety problem in the first place. These food safety issues and others—such as the debates about food technologies, mad cow disease, high-fructose corn syrup, and pesticides—are explored in *Introducing Issues with Opposing Viewpoints: Food Safety.*

Notes
1. Center for Science in the Public Interest. "Legislation—111th Congress," www.cspinet.org/foodsafety/legislation.html.
2. Margaret A. Hamburg, "Food Safety Modernization Act: Putting the Focus on Prevention," FoodSafety.gov, January 3, 2011. www.foodsafety.gov/news/fsma.html.
3. Quoted in Center for Science in the Public Interest, "President to Sign Historic Food Safety Bill, Reforming FDA," January 3, 2011. www.cspinet.org/new/201101032.html.
4. Quoted in Center for Science in the Public Interest, "President to Sign Historic Food Safety Bill, Reforming FDA."
5. Len Steiner, "Look Before Crossing, Cook Before Consuming," *Food Safety News*, February 1, 2011. www.foodsafetynews.com/2011/02/look-before-crossing-cook-before-consuming.

6. Anastacia Marx de Salcedo, "Five Food Safety Myths—Debunked!," *Need to Know*, February 8, 2011. www.pbs.org/wnet/need-to-know/the-daily-need/five-food-safety-myths-debunked/7132.

7. Mike Adams, "How the Food Safety Modernization Act Will Destroy American Jobs, Farms, and Local Foods," NaturalNews.com, January 12, 2011. www.naturalnews.com/030986_food_safety_farmers.html.

8. Quoted in "FDA Looks for Ways to Fund $1.4 Billion Food Safety Reform Act," Homeland Security Newswire, January 20, 2011. http://homelandsecuritynewswire.com/fda-looks-ways-fund-14-billion-food-safety-reform-act.

Chapter 1

Does the Current US System Ensure Food Safety?

The US Department of Agriculture and the Food and Drug Administration are responsible for food inspections in the United States.

Viewpoint 1

Food Is Safer than It Has Ever Been

Robert Paarlberg

In the following viewpoint Robert Paarlberg argues that food in the United States is very safe and much safer than it was in the past. He contends that it may seem otherwise because of the media attention given to stories about food-borne illness. Paarlberg claims that most instances of food-borne illness are the result of improper handling, not due to the contamination of foods bought at the supermarket. Paarlberg explains how food safety is regulated in the United States and how food safety has become a political issue, which he claims is partially related to an increase in imported food. Paarlberg is the Betty Freyhof Johnson Class of 1944 Professor of Political Science at Wellesley College and an associate at the Weatherhead Center for International Affairs at Harvard University. He is the author of *Food Politics: What Everyone Needs to Know* and *Starved for Science: How Biotechnology Is Being Kept Out of Africa.*

> *"America's food supply is far safer today than it was in the past."*

Robert Paarlberg, "Food Safety and Genetically Engineered Foods," in *Food Politics: What Everyone Needs to Know,* New York: Oxford University Press, 2010, pp. 155–159. By permission of Oxford University Press, Inc.

AS YOU READ, CONSIDER THE FOLLOWING QUESTIONS:
1. Paarlberg claims that the Centers for Disease Control and Prevention found that food-borne diseases cause how many deaths each year in the United States?
2. At what year does the author claim that aggregate food safety in the United States hit a plateau?
3. What two government agencies are responsible for US food safety, according to the author?

Food in the United States is generally safe and significantly safer than in the past, but the demand for safety has increased as society has become more affluent, creating a parallel demand for improved food safety policy. Food safety lapses are favorite stories in the popular media, and food companies and food retailers can pay a heavy price if the lapse is traced back to them.

Food-Borne Illness

More than 200 known diseases can be transmitted through food, caused primarily by viruses, bacteria, parasites, toxins, metals, or prions (as in the case of mad cow disease). The symptoms can range from mild gastroenteritis to life-threatening neurologic, hepatic, and renal syndromes. According to the Centers for Disease Control and Prevention (CDC) in Atlanta, Georgia, food-borne diseases cause approximately 325,000 hospitalizations and 5,000 deaths in the United States each year. Three pathogens, *Salmonella*, *Listeria*, and *Toxoplasma*, are responsible for approximately 30 percent of the deaths. Children under the age of 4 are sickened by food more than any other age group, but adults over the age of 50 suffer more hospitalizations and deaths.

The changing frequency of food-borne illness in any large population is difficult to monitor and measure. Mild cases often go unreported, so official frequency counts are heavily altered by the intensity of surveillance. Nationally since 1996, the CDC has attempted to track food-borne sickness through regular surveys of more than 650 clinical laboratories around the country that serve about 46 million people in 10 different states. At the state level, however, surveillance is less systematic and produces counts that are hard to compare. For example, between 1990 and 2006, the state of Minnesota discovered 548 food-borne illness outbreaks thanks to an aggressive surveillance system, but the state of Kentucky found only 18. Kentucky's food supply was almost certainly not that much safer, if it was safer at all. In some cases, food-borne illness can also be overreported because many pathogens transmitted by food are also spread through water or from person to person without anything being ingested at all. In many cases, the specific pathogens are never identified, creating a further possibility that the illness was unrelated to food.

An Increase in Food Safety

America's food supply is far safer today than it was in the past, before the era of refrigeration and sanitary packaging. Surveys by the CDC show decades of steadily increasing safety up until 2005, at which point aggregate food safety in the United States reached something of a plateau. One possible explanation for the plateau is that nearly all the easy measures waiting to be taken outside the home had already been taken. The vast majority of all hospitalizations and fatalities today come not from specific outbreaks linked to dangerous batches of contaminated products purchased at supermarkets but instead from a steady background level of illness caused by careless handling and improper preparation inside the home. Unwashed hands, unwashed cutting boards, poorly refrigerated foods, or meats insufficiently cooked can all present serious dangers. Wider illness outbreaks still take place, but the fatalities are usually quite limited. Illness from bagged spinach in 2006 led to a nationwide scare and the virtual suspension of all fresh and bagged spinach sales in America, but there were only three known deaths.

FAST FACT

A century ago typhoid fever, tuberculosis, and cholera were common food-borne diseases, but due to improvements in food safety, those diseases have been conquered.

Even if the CDC number of 5,000 annual deaths from food-borne illness is accurate, this is far fewer than from smoking (400,000

Estimated Frequency of Food-borne Illness in the United States

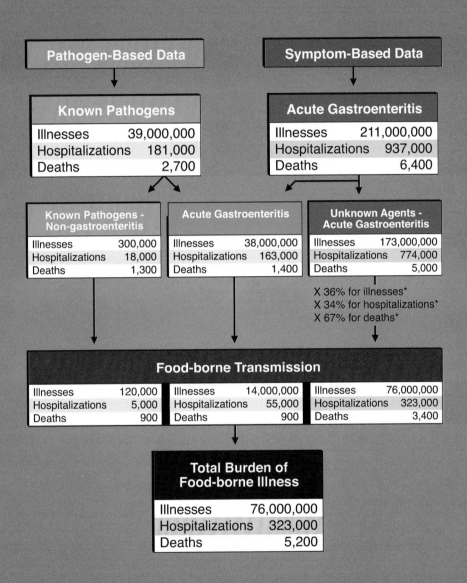

| Pathogen-Based Data | | Symptom-Based Data | |

Known Pathogens

Illnesses	39,000,000
Hospitalizations	181,000
Deaths	2,700

Acute Gastroenteritis

Illnesses	211,000,000
Hospitalizations	937,000
Deaths	6,400

Known Pathogens - Non-gastroenteritis

Illnesses	300,000
Hospitalizations	18,000
Deaths	1,300

Acute Gastroenteritis

Illnesses	38,000,000
Hospitalizations	163,000
Deaths	1,400

Unknown Agents - Acute Gastroenteritis

Illnesses	173,000,000
Hospitalizations	774,000
Deaths	5,000

X 36% for illnesses*
X 34% for hospitalizations*
X 67% for deaths*

Food-borne Transmission

Illnesses	120,000	Illnesses	14,000,000	Illnesses	76,000,000
Hospitalizations	5,000	Hospitalizations	55,000	Hospitalizations	323,000
Deaths	900	Deaths	900	Deaths	3,400

Total Burden of Food-borne Illness

Illnesses	76,000,000
Hospitalizations	323,000
Deaths	5,200

*Percentages derived from observed frequency of food-borne transmission of acute gastroenteritis caused by known pathogens.

Taken from: Centers for Disease Control and Prevention, "Food-Related Illness and Death in the United States," Atlanta, Georgia, USA, October 25, 2005.

Americans a year) or even from obesity (30,000 Americans a year). Note that too much food is now six times deadlier than unsafe food. Yet any illness from foods found already contaminated at purchase will cause public outrage because (in contrast to smoking or overeating) this kind of exposure to risk is involuntary. Also, because purchasing food at supermarkets is a common experience, anxieties can spread quickly to vast numbers of citizens when any danger associated with food purchase is confirmed or even rumored. The unusually wide audience for these fears explains why the popular media give food illness outbreaks from product contamination such sensational coverage. Under the spotlight of this media attention, government officials and politicians find themselves obliged to express intense concern, whatever the actual magnitude of the problem. . . .

The Regulation of Food

At the federal level, food safety responsibility is divided between the Food and Drug Administration [FDA] (an office of the U.S. Department of Health and Human Services) and the Food Safety and Inspection Service (FSIS), which operates inside the Department of Agriculture. The FSIS is responsible for meat and poultry, and the FDA is responsible for everything else. State public health agencies and city and county health departments also play a continuous monitoring role. Inadequate coordination among these various agencies is a cause for political concern. In 1998, the Clinton administration created a Food Outbreak Response Coordinating Group inside the Department of Health and Human Services, designed to increase communication and coordination. The division of labor between the FSIS and the FDA is particularly problematic. For example, frozen pizzas are inspected by the FDA if they are cheese and by the FSIS if they are pepperoni.

The FDA budget for food inspections is also a partisan issue, with Democrats calling for an increase and Republicans proposing cuts. It is also a problem that the FDA is responsible for both food safety and drug safety, and some have called for a separate agency to oversee food safety exclusively. By 2009, more than a half-dozen food safety policy overhaul bills had been filed in Congress, most designed to give the FDA more financing and greater legal authority to recall unsafe food from the market even without a manufacturer's consent. In 2009, the House of Representatives passed new legislation that contained such a measure and required the FDA to conduct inspections every 6 to 12 months at food processing plants deemed to be high risk. President Barack Obama had described the government's failure to inspect 95 percent of food processing plants as "a hazard to the public health."

Some of this political concern is driven by a dramatic increase in the consumption of imported food. According to the FDA, the volume of FDA-regulated imports doubled between 2003–2008, and 60 percent of these imported shipments were food. Approximately 15 percent of the U.S. food supply is now imported, with the import share for fresh fruits and seafood reaching 50–60 percent of total

The Centers for Disease Control and Prevention (CDC) reports that three pathogens, Salmonella (shown), Listeria, and Toxoplasma are responsible for 30 percent of the five thousand deaths that occur each year due to food-borne diseases.

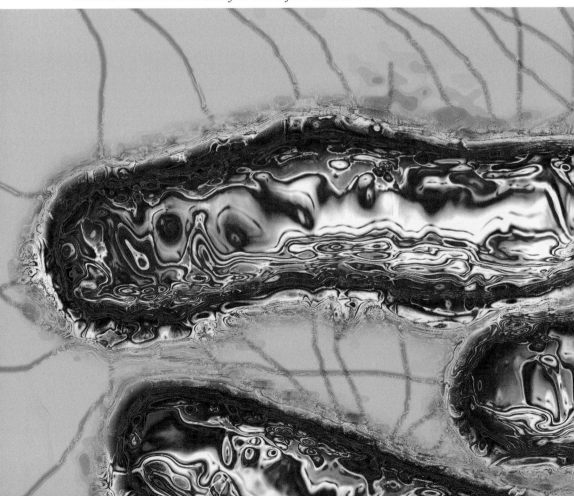

supply. The FDA can physically inspect less than 1 percent of all food imports because funding levels for this activity were cut by 20 percent between 2002–08. Inspections for high-risk food facilities, including fresh produce firms, declined by a quarter after 2004. The presence of such gaps in government inspection did not prove food had become less safe, but it did fuel intense public suspicion.

EVALUATING THE AUTHOR'S ARGUMENTS:

In this viewpoint Robert Paarlberg notes that the official counts of food-borne illness are influenced by the intensity of surveillance. Nonetheless, Paarlberg claims that food in the United States has never been safer. How might Ken Foskett, the author of the following viewpoint, use Paarlberg's claim about surveillance to disagree with his conclusion about food safety?

The Food Safety System in America Is Substandard

Ken Foskett

"The FDA's inspection record underscores the need for more regular, comprehensive food inspections."

In the following viewpoint Ken Foskett contends that the food safety network in America is inefficient and not up to standard. Foskett claims that one of the main problems is that the US Food and Drug Administration (FDA) operates under food safety standards that are primarily voluntary. Foskett argues that uniform safety standards are needed, along with mandated uniform safety protocols for certain foods. Foskett also claims that the FDA needs to perform more inspections with more highly skilled inspectors. He emphasizes that changes to the food safety system need to prioritize prevention rather than crisis management. Foskett is opinion editor for the *Atlanta Journal-Constitution*, having also worked at the publication as a Washington correspondent, statehouse reporter, science writer, and investigative reporter.

AS YOU READ, CONSIDER THE FOLLOWING QUESTIONS:
1. According to Foskett, Food and Drug Administration inspectors visit every food processor in America how often?
2. The salmonella outbreak at the Peanut Corporation of America affected at least how many products, according to the author?
3. Foskett claims that in the 1970s food processing plants received a visit from the Food and Drug Administration approximately how often?

A mericans eat food imported from 150 foreign countries and processed in 189,000 plants scattered from China to Fiji. In 2007, the Food and Drug Administration [FDA] inspected 96 of those plants.

An Inefficient Food Safety Network

Here in the United States, FDA inspectors visit every food processor about once every 10 years, a record that makes its recent inspection of the Peanut Corporation of America plant in Blakely [Georgia] something of a coup.

The FDA had last been to Blakely in 2001; when it returned in January [2009] in response to a crisis, it found salmonella on plant surfaces, peanuts stored under water leaks, dead roaches and unidentified "slimy, black-brown residue." By that time, authorities had already identified the Peanut Corp. plant as the likely source of salmonella-contaminated peanut butter that so far [as of March 1, 2009] has killed nine Americans and sickened more than 660.

The FDA's inspection record underscores the need for more regular, comprehensive food inspections. But it also speaks to the importance of prevention and transparency, not crisis management, in protecting the safety of our food supply.

An efficient safety network prevents contamination before food products are shipped to schools, senior centers and grocery stores. An efficient system also tracks illness outbreaks quickly and recalls tainted products with equal speed.

Today, the U.S. food-safety network does not meet those standards, and Americans are literally dying as a result.

The Peanut Corporation Scandal

Lou Tousignant's father, a decorated Korean War veteran, died in a nursing home after eating contaminated peanut butter from Georgia.

"How can we live in the United States of America where a man literally gave his blood, sweat and tears for his country?" his son asked U.S. House members this month [March 2009]. "How can we live in a country that . . . let him down?"

The breakdowns at Peanut Corp.'s Georgia plant illustrate the failures of an entire system. The plant's food-safety protocol, drafted by the company, was so haphazard that the equipment used to make peanut butter wasn't cleaned even after company tests found salmonella.

Company officials repeatedly shipped peanuts that they knew were contaminated by salmonella and didn't tell anyone. Under the law, they didn't have to.

Once shipped, the contaminated peanuts circulated for weeks before regulators could identify products implicated, a list now numbering 2,100 and growing. Ultimately, FDA inspectors had to invoke bioterrorism laws to gain access to Peanut Corp.'s records, and under

When the Peanut Corporation of America plant in Blakely, Georgia, was inspected by the FDA for the first time in eight years the inspectors found salmonella, peanuts stored under water leaks, dead roaches, and an unidentified "slimy, black-brown residue."

the law it had to ask the company's permission to seek a recall of its tainted products.

No other industry, especially one that so directly affects health and wellness, operates under so many voluntary safety standards. Apart from basic sanitary procedures, FDA safety standards for most food products are voluntary, the result of food companies demanding the flexibility to pick and choose protocols that work best for them.

The fallacy of this argument, as the Peanut Corp. fiasco clearly shows, is that some companies will pick and choose to do nothing at all.

In the past, the food industry has fended off calls for tougher mandatory standards by arguing that it's unfair to penalize the good players because of the mistakes of the bad.

But many good companies have been seriously harmed by the Peanut Corp. scandal. For those firms that used Peanut Corp. products and counted on the company to ensure safety—companies such as Kellogg, the maker of Keebler cookies, and Publix, which used Peanut Corp. products for its store-brand snack bars—that damage is direct. For the peanut industry as a whole, the damage to public confidence in its product is indirect but no doubt longer-lasting.

The Need for Safety Protocols

Congress must give the FDA the authority to mandate uniform safety standards for all types of food. In certain industries, the FDA must also go a step further and require companies to implement HACCP protocols for high-risk foods.

HACCP, or Hazard Analysis Critical Control Points, is a proven safety protocol that requires processors to analyze potential contamination risks, develop a safety plan and regularly document how its processes are working, including periodic testing.

Salmonella Infections Associated with Peanut Butter and Peanut Butter–Containing Products—United States, 2008–2009

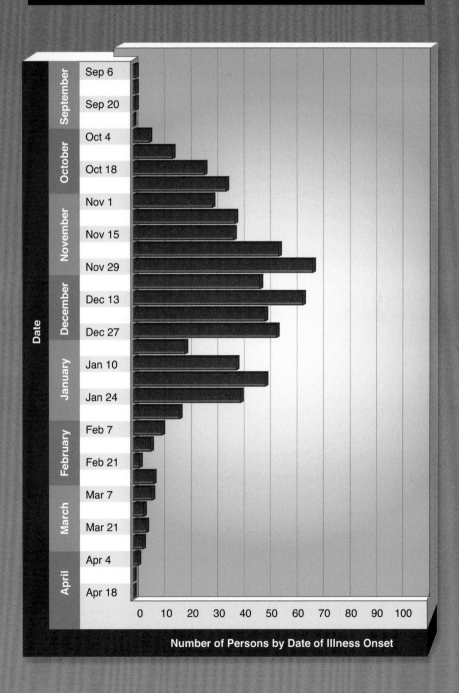

Taken from: Centers for Disease Prevention and Control (CDC), "2008–2009 Salmonella Typhimurium Outbreak Response," After Action Report; May 18, 2009.

As Georgia and FDA regulators point out, inspections show only how safely a plant is operating on the inspection day. HACCP procedures generate regular reports on how equipment is functioning—is the peanut roaster hot enough to kill germs, for example. Inspectors can then review those documents for the preceding six months, giving them a peek into plant operations over the long haul, not just that day.

At a minimum, the FDA should require HACCP procedures for fresh produce, which accounts for the greatest number of food-borne illnesses behind seafood.

The FDA must also step up efforts to trace food, particularly raw foods such as peanuts and produce that get blended in the food supply and become difficult to trace back to their point of origin.

Even though the list of brands contaminated by Peanut Corp. peanuts is now widely known, for example, regulators can't say with certainty that all of them have been taken off shelves. We bar-code meats; why not peanut lots and lettuce?

The Need for Increased Inspection

Congress also needs to give the FDA more money for inspectors. In the 1970s, the FDA inspected 35,000 plants a year, each one about every other year. Today, with staff reductions and more facilities to monitor, it gets to each plant every decade or so.

The FDA also counts heavily on 30,000 inspectors working for state and local governments, whose qualifications vary widely. To address the training gap, the W.K. Kellogg Foundation is launching a National Food Protection Center in Michigan to offer the same type of career-spanning training that peace officers receive at the Federal Law Enforcement Training Center in Georgia. Congress should support such initiatives.

In Georgia, quick action is needed on Senate legislation requiring food processors to test their products regularly and notify regulators immediately when "finished" food products test positive for a contaminant. Processors can follow a testing regimen mandated by the state or submit their own food-safety plan for state approval.

However, it's uncertain how long it would take agriculture officials to approve thousands of new food safety plans or where the agency will get the resources to do it.

As they address those and similar questions, members of Congress and the state Legislature should reread Lou Tousignant's congressional testimony about his father. No nation should fail its citizens the way the United States failed his father.

EVALUATING THE AUTHOR'S ARGUMENTS:

In this viewpoint Ken Foskett focuses his discussion of food safety on the peanut contamination and talks about a war veteran who died from the contamination. What might Robert Paarlberg, the author of the previous viewpoint, say about Foskett's focus on this outbreak?

More Government Regulation Is Needed to Ensure Food Safety

"The economic case for having the government enforce rules on food safety seems over-whelming."

Paul Krugman

In the following viewpoint Paul Krugman contends that at the root of the food safety crisis in America is a flawed ideology that rejects government regulation. Krugman admits that part of the food-safety problem is due to the inability to inspect all foreign food-processing plants, part is due to lack of transparency by food corporations, and part is due to the failure of the government to implement new regulations unless the private sector wants them. But behind all of this, Krugman says, is the real culprit: the conservative ideology that insists the private sector should police itself in all situations, without government regulation. He concludes that this ideology must be abandoned as it applies to food producers and that the government must enforce stronger rules on food safety. Krugman is a columnist for the *New York Times* and a professor of economics and international affairs at Princeton University.

AS YOU READ, CONSIDER THE FOLLOWING QUESTIONS:
1. According to Krugman, when it comes to imported food, American consumers are dependent on what for food safety?
2. Krugman claims that the US Food and Drug Administration has introduced no significant new food regulations since what year?
3. Who does Krugman charge with legitimizing the ideology that he claims is responsible for the food safety crisis in America?

Yesterday I did something risky: I ate a salad.

The New Fear of Eating

These are anxious days at the lunch table. For all you know, there may be E. coli on your spinach, salmonella in your peanut butter and melamine in your pet's food and, because it was in the feed, in your chicken sandwich.

Who's responsible for the new fear of eating? Some blame globalization; some blame food-producing corporations; some blame the [George W.] Bush administration. But I blame [American economist] Milton Friedman.

Now, those who blame globalization do have a point. U.S. officials can't inspect overseas food-processing plants without the permission of foreign governments—and since the Food and Drug Administration has limited funds and manpower, it can inspect only a small percentage of imports. This leaves American consumers effectively dependent on the quality of foreign food-safety enforcement. And that's not a healthy place to be, especially when it comes to imports from China, where the state of food safety is roughly what it was in this country before the Progressive movement.

The Washington Post, reviewing F.D.A. documents, found that last month [April 2007] the agency detained shipments from China that included dried apples treated with carcinogenic chemicals and seafood "coated with putrefying bacteria." You can be sure that a lot of similarly unsafe and disgusting food ends up in American stomachs.

The Lack of Food Safety Regulations

Those who blame corporations also have a point. In 2005, the F.D.A. suspected that peanut butter produced by ConAgra, which sells the product under multiple brand names, might be contaminated with salmonella. According to the *New York Times*, "when agency inspectors went to the plant that made the peanut butter, the company acknowledged it had destroyed some product but declined to say why," and refused to let the inspectors examine its records without a written authorization.

According to the company, the agency never followed through. This brings us to our third villain, the Bush administration.

Without question, America's food safety system has degenerated over the past six years [2001–2007]. We don't know how many times concerns raised by F.D.A. employees were ignored or soft-pedaled by their superiors. What we do know is that since 2001 the F.D.A. has introduced no significant new food safety regulations except those mandated by Congress.

This isn't simply a matter of caving in to industry pressure. The Bush administration won't issue food safety regulations even when the private sector wants them. The president of the United Fresh Produce Association says that the industry's problems "can't be solved without strong mandatory federal regulations": without such regulations, scrupulous growers and processors risk being undercut by competitors more willing to cut corners on food safety. Yet the administration refuses to do more than issue nonbinding guidelines.

> **FAST FACT**
>
> Milton Friedman (1912–2006) was a well-known American economist who developed a philosophy promoting free market economics and opposing government regulation, which has influenced conservatives.

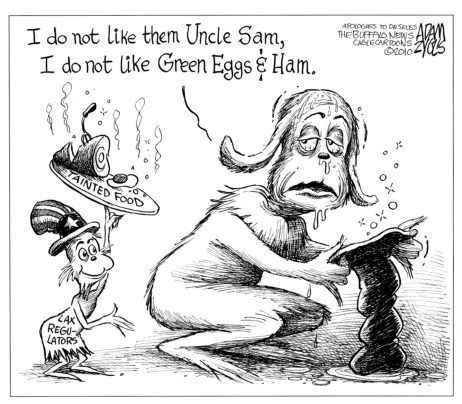

I do not like them Uncle Sam,
I do not like Green Eggs & Ham.

APOLOGIES TO DR.SEUSS
THE BUFFALO NEWS
CAGLECARTOONS
©2010

ADAM ZYGLIS

TAINTED FOOD

LAX REGU-LATORS

A Sickening Ideology

Why would the administration refuse to regulate an industry that actually wants to be regulated? Officials may fear that they would create a precedent for public-interest regulation of other industries. But they are also influenced by an ideology that says business should never be regulated, no matter what.

The economic case for having the government enforce rules on food safety seems overwhelming. Consumers have no way of knowing whether the food they eat is contaminated, and in this case what you don't know can hurt or even kill you. But there are some people who refuse to accept that case, because it's ideologically inconvenient. That's why I blame the food safety crisis on Milton Friedman, who called for the abolition of both the food and the drug sides of the F.D.A. What would protect the public from dangerous or ineffective drugs? "It's in the self-interest of pharmaceutical companies not to have these bad things," he insisted in a 1999 interview. He would

Milton Friedman was a Nobel Prize winner in economics who promoted free-market economics.

presumably have applied the same logic to food safety (as he did to airline safety): regardless of circumstances, you can always trust the private sector to police itself.

O.K., I'm not saying that Mr. Friedman directly caused tainted spinach and poisonous peanut butter. But he did help to make our food less safe, by legitimizing what the historian Rick Perlstein calls

"E. coli conservatives": ideologues who won't accept even the most compelling case for government regulation.

Earlier this month the administration named, you guessed it, a "food safety czar." But the food safety crisis isn't caused by the arrangement of the boxes on the organization chart. It's caused by the dominance within our government of a literally sickening ideology.

EVALUATING THE AUTHOR'S ARGUMENTS:

In this viewpoint Paul Krugman worries that consumers have no way to know whether they are eating contaminated food. Arthur E. Foulkes, the author of the following viewpoint, claims that this is a version of the asymmetric information argument and draws analogies with what three beneficial market exchanges to support its harmlessness?

Viewpoint

4

Government Regulation Is Not the Best Way to Ensure Food Safety

"To dismiss the fact that companies have an incentive not to harm their consumers and imply that only government officials can do this . . . is to leave out an important part of the food-safety picture."

Arthur E. Foulkes

In the following viewpoint Arthur E. Foulkes argues that it is false that government regulation is the best way to address food safety. Foulkes claims that even though food consumers have less information about food safety than food producers do, this does not mean that government regulation is the best way to fill this gap. Foulkes claims that food sellers have an inherent incentive to make food safe. When food corporations are not entirely transparent about food safety issues, it could be to protect proprietary information rather than any sinister motive, he claims. Foulkes warns that just because industry wants regulation does not mean that that is a good reason for government to step in, as the demand for regulation is often unrelated to food safety. Foulkes is a research fellow at the Independent Institute and a writer for the *Terre Haute Tribune-Star* in Indiana.

AS YOU READ, CONSIDER THE FOLLOWING QUESTIONS:
1. What four examples does Foulkes give of private means of assurance that exist to address asymmetric information?
2. The author claims that sellers of imported food have an important incentive to do what?
3. What two pieces of legislation does Foulkes give as examples of government food regulation that he says were pushed by businesses for reasons other than food safety?

There is a "food safety crisis" in America and Milton Friedman is to blame, Princeton University economist Paul Krugman wrote on the *New York Times* op-ed page May 21 [2007]. Friedman is responsible, Krugman wrote, because he legitimized a "sickening ideology" that rejects "even the most compelling" cases for government regulation of business.

Krugman's "crisis" stems from several recent incidents with tainted food, including *E. coli* in spinach in 2006, which led to three deaths and several illnesses; salmonella in peanut butter; and melamine in pet food. More recently, food imported from China has caused concern.

The Asymmetric Information Argument

He believes the government needs to guarantee food safety because market forces alone cannot. His case, however, both understates the ability of the market to provide food-quality assurance and disregards or ignores important arguments against relying on the government for this purpose.

Krugman writes that "the economic case" for government food-safety regulation is "overwhelming" because people buying food know much less about its quality than sellers do. This is the "asymmetric information" argument common in market-failure literature.

Yet asymmetric information problems are not unusual. For example, when I am hired, I know more about my work habits than the person doing the hiring. When I purchase auto insurance, I know more about my driving skills than the insurer. When I buy a lamp, I know far less about its quality than the manufacturer. Yet despite all this, somehow we engage in mutually beneficial exchanges every day.

Indeed, the existence of asymmetric information creates a market for assurance services that entrepreneurs quickly fill. Examples of private means of assurance range from neighborhood gossip to trusted brand names to Underwriters Laboratories to *Consumer Reports.*

Brand names provide an informal means of quality assurance that companies and consumers are willing to pay for. Likewise, middlemen, such as department or grocery stores, also provide a reputation-conscious source of quality assurance that both consumers and producers are willing to pay for.

Food may be potentially more dangerous than many other goods, but this fact only adds to the incentives for private assurance. Indeed, a downside to using the government for food-quality assurance, such as the Food and Drug Administration (FDA), is that it makes consumers less conscious of food safety in general. Furthermore, the existence of the FDA "crowds out" private (and more creative) assurance providers that would certainly emerge in its absence.

The Incentive Not to Harm

Krugman worries about Americans buying so much food from abroad, pointing out darkly that FDA inspectors check only a tiny percentage of the imports. This leaves the American consumer "dependent on the quality of foreign food-safety enforcement," he writes.

Yet government food inspectors are not really the only source of quality assurance for imported food. Even though Krugman dismisses this point in his piece, sellers of imported food really do have an important incentive to avoid making their customers sick.

"The food industry bristles at the notion that a greater diversity of foreign ingredient suppliers could increase risks for consumers," the *New York Times* reported on June 16 [2007]. "Executives at food companies say that they willingly bear the burden of ensuring the safety of their suppliers' plants and products." The same article quotes an executive at Sara Lee saying, "[Food safety is] on us. We can't sit around and wait for government to iron these things out."

Of course, it is always possible for bad food to reach consumers. There will always be accidents and negligence in any human endeavor. Nevertheless, to dismiss the fact that companies have an incentive not to harm their consumers and imply that only government officials can do this, as Krugman does, is to leave out an important part of the food-safety picture.

The Behavior of Corporations

Krugman also writes that corporations are at fault in the food crisis, citing salmonella contamination in ConAgra peanut butter that came to light in 2005. Krugman also notes that ConAgra officials, during a surprise two-day FDA inspection prompted by an anonymous tip about the contamination, refused to hand over company documents without a written request from the FDA.

ConAgra has said that their own routine inspections in the plant found the contaminated peanut butter before it ever left the plant, making government inspections unnecessary.

Percent of people responding "excellent" or "pretty good" when rating the job this federal government agency does.

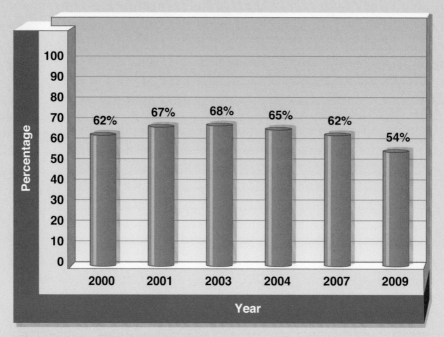

Taken from: Harris Interactive poll, January 12–19, 2009.

While this certainly shows corporations can have food-safety problems, it may not be a persuasive case of corporate irresponsibility. ConAgra detected the salmonella during its own routine inspections and, a spokeswoman told me, none of the contaminated peanut butter ever left the company's control or reached consumers.

As for why ConAgra refused to hand over documents without a written request, the spokeswoman said it wanted to be sure it handed over all the requested information and to keep any of its "proprietary information" from becoming part of the public record.

Some people will see something sinister in anything a corporation does, but in this case at least, the company seems to have responded effectively to the problem and acted reasonably when dealing with a surprise government inspection.

The Argument That Industry Wants Regulation

Krugman also blames the Bush administration for the food crisis because it refuses to regulate private industries even when they ask for it. He quotes the president of a food-industry group calling for stronger government regulations.

Yet it is not unusual for business people to seek government regulations, nor does this demonstrate that the sought regulations are in the public's interest. Often business people want regulations to cripple competitors or restore public confidence at taxpayer expense. The Meat Inspection Acts of 1891 and 1906 provide good examples.

Refrigeration changed the meatpacking industry dramatically in the late 1800s, allowing large centralized packers in Chicago to offer meat in greater quantities and at lower costs than before. Threatened by the new competition, smaller local slaughterhouses began to claim the Chicago packers were unsanitary. Demand for meat fell (along with prices)—leading the industry to ask for federal regulations to restore public confidence. The result was the Meat Inspection Act of 1891.

A similar situation led to passage of the Meat Inspection Act of 1906 as well. As Lawrence Reed has written, big meatpackers "got the taxpayers to pick up the entire $3 million price tag for [the Meat Inspection Act's] implementation." They also got new regulations placed on their smaller competitors.

Finally, Krugman's essay overlooks an important economic argument against the FDA itself. Economists have long understood that because of the perverse incentives its employees face, the agency weighs decisions heavily on the side of caution. As a result, it has often kept lifesaving drugs and products off the market at the cost of many thousands of lives.

Increased Inspection of Imported Food Is Necessary for Safety

Diana Furchtgott-Roth

> *"Consumers would be wise to support measures that would increase food safety."*

In the following viewpoint Diana Furchtgott-Roth argues that there is not enough being done to ensure the safety of imported food to the United States. She contends that most imported food products are not tested for contamination and most foreign food processing plants are not inspected. Furchtgott-Roth proposes that the US Food and Drug Administration be given the resources and authority to monitor a higher percentage of imported foods and to inspect foreign businesses. She also believes that food importers need to have better standards of accountability. Furchtgott-Roth concludes that legislation to increase the safety of imported food in the above ways should be supported. Furchtgott-Roth is a senior fellow at the Hudson Institute and a former chief economist at the US Department of Labor.

AS YOU READ, CONSIDER THE FOLLOWING QUESTIONS:

1. According to Furchtgott-Roth, what happened when US inspectors were finally given visas to inspect the Chinese factory suspected of producing contaminated pet food?
2. What are the respective budgets of the US Department of Agriculture (USDA) and the US Food and Drug Administration (FDA), according to the author?
3. Furchtgott-Roth supports the passage of legislation that would authorize how much more spending for the USDA and FDA to monitor imports?

W hile parents are trying to avoid placing Chinese-made toys such as Aqua Dots, assembled with a toxic glue, and Thomas the Tank Engines that are painted with lead under the Christmas tree, there is a potentially greater challenge: ensuring the safety of imported foods their children and all of us eat every day.

The Safety of Imported Food

This year [2007] Americans will buy about $14 billion worth of fruits and vegetables imported from all countries, with a majority of imports coming from Mexico, Canada, and Chile. That's 75% more than a decade ago and 42% more than five years ago. Purchases of imported meat, poultry, eggs, and dairy products are up 65% over the past decade.

Americans have high expectations about the safety of their food supply, domestic and imported. They expect the government to do a thorough review of it. If something goes wrong, they also expect the government to fix the problem. When an outbreak of E. coli occurred in October 2006, government scientists not only found that it originated in packaged spinach but also discovered the precise field in California where the spinach was grown.

Unfortunately such high expectations cannot be applied to imported foods. Sources of foods are farther away, and some governments don't want American inspectors poking around processing plants and farms.

Public Opinion on FDA Inspection of Foreign Food Production Facilities

The FDA inspects food-processing facilities periodically.

Approximately how often do you feel the FDA should conduct its inspections of foreign food-processing facilities?

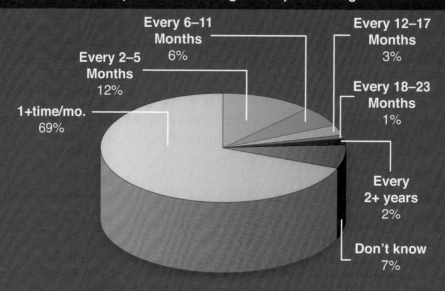

Every 6–11 Months 6%

Every 12–17 Months 3%

Every 2–5 Months 12%

1+time/mo. 69%

Every 18–23 Months 1%

Every 2+ years 2%

Don't know 7%

Taken from: Consumer Reports National Research Center, "Food-Labeling Poll 2008," November 11, 2008.

Just look at last April's [2007] pet food scandal. It turns out that Chinese producers deliberately mixed toxic melanine with wheat flour to give the appearance of wheat gluten, which has a higher protein content and is more valuable. The melanine in pet foods was discovered only accidentally, when an American pet food company taste-tested two types of food on cats, and one group died.

Initially, China refused to let American inspectors into the country to visit the pet food factory. By the time the inspectors were given visas, the factory had been bull-dozed to the ground.

Given the millions of farms and factories worldwide that export to America, and the frequency of terrorist threats, it's remarkable how few food-related problems we have.

Oversight of America's Food Supply

Our government does a thorough job of inspecting meat. The U.S. Department of Agriculture [USDA] inspects meat, poultry, and eggs, produced both domestically and abroad. On the Agriculture Department's Web site there is a list, by country, of factories permitted to export to America. These factories adhere to American standards and are subject to periodic inspections.

Congress gives the Agriculture Department $925 million to oversee one-fifth of America's food supply that is based on animal products. The other four-fifths are under the scrutiny of the Food and Drug Administration [FDA], which is part of the Department of Health and Human Services, whose appropriation for food safety is only $385 million.

There is a mismatch here. FDA needs more money. FDA has the resources to check only 1% of food imported to America. That's a woefully small sample when we're engaged in a war with radical Muslim fundamentalists who call us "The Great Satan" and who don't blink at crashing planes into the World Trade Center, much less contaminating our food supply.

> **FAST FACT**
>
> In 2007 the US Food and Drug Administration received reports that approximately two thousand cats and two thousand dogs died as a result of eating contaminated pet food from China.

According to a former associate commissioner of the FDA and an adviser to the Coalition for a Stronger FDA, Bill Hubbard, "If people knew how weak FDA was, they would be shocked." He proposes doubling the FDA's budget, enabling the agency to hire more scientists and inspectors, and sample between 5% and 10% of imported food.

Last month, the FDA put out its Food Protection Plan, which focuses on prevention of contamination, both intentional and accidental. It contains a list of proposed legislative changes, some of which are so basic it's bewildering that Congress hasn't made them already.

For instance, the FDA wants Congressional authorization to prevent the entry of food from foreign businesses that fail to allow inspection by FDA officials. Currently, the FDA cannot refuse admission of food from companies that don't allow their farms or plants to be inspected in FDA's sampling process. The FDA also seeks authority from Congress to "require preventative controls to prevent intentional adulteration by terrorists or criminals at points of high vulnerability in the food chain." For example, it could require locks on tankers or trucks carrying milk that are parked overnight at rest stops.

A man holds a picture of his dog that was poisoned by bad pet food from China. The FDA reported that over two thousand cats and two thousand dogs died as a result of eating contaminated pet food from China.

Proposals to Increase Food Safety

On Tuesday [December 4, 2007], the Senate Committee on Health, Education, Labor and Pensions held hearings on the Food Protection Plan. At the hearing, a professor at the George Washington University School of Public Health, Mike Taylor, testified that the FDA cannot possibly be expected to check thoroughly all food arriving at the border, and that comprehensive industry accountability is needed. Firms who import need to make sure they meet American standards.

The president and CEO [chief executive officer] of the Grocery Manufacturers Association, Cal Dooley, also testified that more accountability is needed. He called for requiring every food importer to put in place a foreign supplier quality program that makes sure all imports meet FDA food safety standards. The multinational food company, Cargill, was independently cited by both Taylor and Hubbard in phone conversations as an example of a company that takes import safety seriously. "They will not buy if they don't know where it's coming from," Mr. Hubbard said.

On Wednesday, Senators Casey and Grassley introduced the EAT SAFE Act, S 2418, which would authorize $31 million more for both the USDA and the FDA to monitor imports. This is a small step in the right direction, although the outlook for passage of this bill is unclear. Fortunately for shoppers who enjoy out-of-season berries at Christmas dinner, Congress is not trying to make us give up imported food in the same way as it wants us give up imported energy. But contamination of the food supply, whether deliberate or accidental, can be lethal. Consumers would be wise to support measures that would increase food safety.

EVALUATING THE AUTHOR'S ARGUMENTS:

In this viewpoint Diana Furchtgott-Roth emphasizes the need for more inspections and oversight to guarantee the safety of imported food. How does the solution proposed by Kevin A. Hassett, the author of the following viewpoint, differ? On what point(s) do they agree?

Viewpoint

6

Transparency About Imported Food Is Necessary for Safety

Kevin A. Hassett

"It is intolerable that consumers have no way to check where their products come from."

In the following viewpoint Kevin A. Hassett argues that transparency about the country of origin of food products is necessary. Hassett recounts recent experiences with contaminated Chinese food imports in order to make the case for more transparency in labeling. He contends that it is impossible to inspect all food imports, so the United States ought to require that food imports be labeled with their country of origin. Hassett concludes that consumers should ultimately be able to track the origin of all foods in the products they buy. Hassett is a resident scholar and director of economic policy studies at the American Enterprise Institute.

AS YOU READ, CONSIDER THE FOLLOWING QUESTIONS:

1. According to Hassett, the US Food and Drug Administration (FDA) can inspect only what percentage of imports?
2. The author claims that approximately how many shipments from China are refused each month in the United States?
3. Hassett wants the FDA to publish what information on the Internet in order to promote transparency?

Homeland security specialists have long been concerned that the U.S.'s food chain may be a prime target for terrorists. The recent experience with foodstuffs and medicines from China suggests these fears are well-founded.

Unscrupulous and poorly regulated Chinese exporters have been shipping poisoned and tainted products at an astonishing rate. These are easily making their way to the American people.

The Dangers of Food Imports

The danger first reached the consciousness of Americans when thousands of pets died because a food additive exported from China and used by many pet-food makers contained a deadly chemical, melamine. Subsequently, the depth of the problem has become clearer, and we've learned that pets aren't the only ones at risk.

The worst case, so far, occurred in Panama, where more than 100 people died from consuming cough syrup laced with a chemical commonly used in antifreeze. Toothpaste has been tainted as well, prompting the U.S. Food and Drug Administration [FDA] to ban imports of that product from China.

Drugs aren't the only issue. The food supply in the U.S. has been found to be awash in questionable products. The FDA can inspect only a bit more than 1 percent of imports shipped to our country, but the defects discovered even in this relatively loose monitoring exercise are almost surreal.

Products from China labeled as monkfish, for example, were found to contain high levels of a toxin that comes from the deadly pufferfish. U.S. distributors issued a massive recall.

Shrimp products from China were found to be contaminated with an antibiotic that is banned in U.S. food products, but that is often used in farms that have unusually filthy water. Thirty-three other shipments of shrimp have been refused because they contained the cancer-causing drug nitrofuran.

Across all foodstuffs, China usually has between 100 and 300 shipments refused each month because of contamination. Given the low monitoring rate, it's a virtual sure thing that tainted foods are consumed every day by Americans.

The Need for Transparency

The level of disregard for human safety by some Chinese manufacturers is amazing. One report aired by National Public Radio found that an herbal tea manufacturer in China was drying its tea leaves by driving trucks back and forth over them, using the hot exhaust as one might a hair dryer.

Pallets of rice are unloaded from a ship docked in the Port of Sacramento. Lack of funding results in the FDA inspecting only 1 percent of the food imports shipped into the country.

This sped up production time and reduced costs. It did so at a big price, however. Since Chinese gasoline contains lead, the tea was tainted by it as well. It is unclear, the report chillingly added, whether the FDA would know to check tea for lead, and unknown whether lead-laden teas have made it into the U.S.

How could it get so bad? One of the biggest problems is that false accusations of food-safety violations are a dime a dozen. Europeans might shun American foodstuffs because they have been genetically modified. The Japanese recently reinstituted a ban on U.S. beef, purportedly because of fears of mad-cow disease.

For a country such as the U.S. that is seeking to expand free global commerce, playing a trade card on foodstuffs opens up a host of potential retributions.

So what should we do? It's not possible to inspect everything that crosses the border. Moreover, the vast majority of Chinese products are probably wholesome.

The right measure would be to simply increase the transparency of agricultural goods and production. If the food you are about to ingest contains substances from China, you ought to be able to find out.

Country-of-Origin Labeling

In 2002, Congress approved a law requiring country-of-origin labeling for various agricultural items—though still not mandating labeling for processed foods containing such commodities. Opponents of the legislation have argued that the cost of keeping track of the origin of every ingredient in their products is exorbitant and that sources can change from month to month, requiring costly new packaging.

Special interests in the U.S. have used their lobbying might to delay the law, and it's now scheduled to take effect in 2008. Those points are probably valid, so here is what Congress should do immediately.

Country-of-Origin Labeling (COOL), Effective January 15, 2009

Who is required to label?

Retail establishments that are licensed under the Perishable Agricultural Commodities Act (PACA) are required to provide COOL information to consumers.

Covered Commodities:

Meat Muscle Cuts

Beef (including veal)
Pork
Lamb
Goat
Chicken

Ground Meat

Beef
Pork
Lamb
Goat
Chicken

Wild and Farm-Raised Fish and Shellfish

Fish
Shellfish

Perishable Agricultural Commodities

Fresh and frozen fruits
Fresh and frozen vegetables

Taken from: United States Department of Agriculture, "COOL Country of Origin Labeling," October 2009.

Anything ingested by Americans and sold in stores should have an identification number on it that cites the batch of the product. Firms should be required to keep track of the countries of origin of every ingredient in every product they make, and to register that information with the FDA. The FDA should then publish that information on the Internet for all to see.

So, if someone wants to know whether a product contains some ingredient from China, he can enter the product code and look. After that, each consumer can weigh the costs and risks, and decide whether to purchase the product.

The Web site should also connect this information to FDA monitoring data. If Chinese shrimp has been found to be suspect often, but Chinese sprouts have not, then this information could be flagged online. Search filters could identify high-risk products. That way, the responsible Chinese sprout growers wouldn't suffer because of the behavior of shrimpers.

It is unacceptable that so much tainted food continues to flow into our country. It is intolerable that consumers have no way to check where their products come from. Congress should act now before the next inevitable crisis hits.

EVALUATING THE AUTHOR'S ARGUMENTS:

In this viewpoint Kevin A. Hassett focuses on the problems with Chinese imports in order to make the case for country-of-origin labeling. Given this, do you think Hassett would be satisfied if only Chinese products were labeled as such? Why or why not?

Chapter 2

Are New Food Technologies Safe?

Workers sort through genetically modified apples. The use of genetically modified foods has caused controversy.

Genetically Modified Biotech Crops Are Safe and Reliable

John Reifsteck

"Biotech crops are the bounty of safe and reliable technologies that deliver environmental and economic sustainability."

In the following viewpoint John Reifsteck argues that biotech crops—those that are genetically modified or genetically engineered—are safe and reliable. Despite criticism to the contrary, Reifsteck claims that rather than increasing the need for pesticides, genetically modified crops need less pesticide. He contends that these biotech crops are one of the most valuable tools for farmers in the ever-evolving management of pests and weeds. Reifsteck concludes that the fact that the vast majority of farmers have adopted genetically modified crops shows that such crops are superior and also supports the idea that they are the new conventional crops. Reifsteck is a corn and soybean farmer in western Champaign County, Illinois, and a board member of Truth About Trade and Technology, a nonprofit advocacy group that supports free trade and agricultural biotechnology.

AS YOU READ, CONSIDER THE FOLLOWING QUESTIONS:
1. Reifsteck cites a study that says that the use of pesticides on global biotech acreage has dropped by what percentage from 1996 to 2009?
2. Which three genetically modified crops does the author identify as having been adopted by the vast majority of farmers?
3. Reifsteck contends that the use of the term *conventional* should be reconsidered when the use of biotechnology rises above what percentage?

Farming is a business. It's my business. Success requires sound business practices. That's why I choose to plant GM [genetically modified] corn and soybeans—and why I'm so appalled by a new activist-sponsored study that questions my ability to make sensible decisions for my own farm.

Biotech Crops and Pesticide Use

Except that this isn't even a "study." To call it that is to insult the test-preparation methods of 10th graders who flunk biology mid-terms. The document issued on Tuesday [November 17, 2009] by three anti-biotech organizations—the Organic Center, the Union of Concerned Scientists, and the Center for Food Safety—is a collection of disputable facts and laughable assertions.

FAST FACT

According to Truth About Trade and Technology, over 2.5 billion biotech crops have been planted and harvested as of the end of 2010.

The central allegation of these groups is that biotech crops are forcing U.S. farmers to use more pesticides. It claims that since 1996, herbicide use is 383 million pounds higher than it would be without GM crops and insecticide use is 64 million pounds lower, for a total increase of 319 million pounds.

First of all, these figures don't tell us much because not all crop protection products are equal. An ounce of one can be more dangerous than a pound of another, so measuring them as if they were all exactly the same is nonsense. Also, it's possible to point to statistics that say the exact opposite. PG Economics Ltd., a well-regarded English consulting firm, recently issued its own findings and said that the use of pesticides on global biotech acreage has dropped almost 800 million pounds—or nearly 9 percent—during the same period.

A genetically modified soybean plant. Ninety-one percent of the soybeans grown today are genetically modified.

production costs—and one of those lower production costs includes less dependence on pesticides.

I can state this as a fact because I've farmed for 37 years. That's another way of saying that I've spent my life battling bugs and weeds. I've used many different tools to protect my crops from destruction—everything from old-fashioned pesticides to new-fangled biotechnology.

Based on my own personal experience—rather than the scare-tactic reports of people who have never laid eyes on my fields—I can say with absolute certainty that biotech crops have allowed me to reduce my pesticide applications.

I know my business, I just wish there weren't so many professional protesters trying to put me out of it.

> ### EVALUATING THE AUTHOR'S ARGUMENTS:
>
> In this viewpoint John Reifsteck focuses on the decline in pesticide use on genetically modified crops. What other concerns are there about genetically modified crops in terms of safety that Reifsteck does not address in this viewpoint?

Genetically Modified Crops Are Not Safe

Institute for Responsible Technology

"There is no monitoring of [genetically modified organism]- related illnesses and no long- term animal studies."

In the following viewpoint the Institute for Responsible Technology argues that there is no science supporting the safety of genetically modified foods. The Institute for Responsible Technology contends that there is evidence that genetically modified foods cause allergies to both the foods themselves and other foods. The author also claims that there is evidence of other health dangers that can result from genetically modified organisms. The Institute for Responsible Technology concludes that many more safety evaluations are needed but cautions that such definitive studies could take many decades to give conclusive evidence of safety, if such studies could guarantee safety at all. The Institute for Responsible Technology is an organization that aims to educate policy makers and the public about genetically modified foods and crops.

AS YOU READ, CONSIDER THE FOLLOWING QUESTIONS:
1. According to the Institute for Responsible Technology, what are the five major genetically modified food crops?
2. The author claims that what happened to the livers of rats fed genetically modified canola?
3. The Institute for Responsible Technology claims that the genetic engineering process used in the production of L-tryptophan caused how many deaths in the 1980s?

In 1992, the Food and Drug Administration claimed they had no information showing that GM [genetically modified] foods were substantially different from conventionally grown foods. Therefore they were safe to eat, and absolutely no safety studies were required. But internal memos made public by a lawsuit reveal that their position was staged by political appointees who were under orders from the White House to promote GMOs [genetically modified organisms]. In addition, the FDA official in charge of creating this policy was Michael Taylor, the former attorney for Monsanto, the largest biotech company, and later their vice president.

The Science of Genetic Engineering

In reality, FDA scientists had repeatedly warned that GM foods can create unpredictable, hard-to-detect side effects, including allergies, toxins, new diseases, and nutritional problems. They urged long-term safety studies, but were ignored.

Today, the same biotech companies who have been found guilty of hiding toxic effects of their chemical products are in charge of determining whether their GM foods are safe. Industry-funded GMO safety studies are too superficial to find most of the potential dangers, and their voluntary consultations with the FDA are widely criticized as a meaningless façade.

Genetic engineering transfers genes across natural species barriers. It uses imprecise laboratory techniques that bear no resemblance to natural breeding, and is based on outdated concepts of how genes and cells work. Gene insertion is done either by shooting genes from a "gene gun" into a plate of cells or by using bacteria to invade the cell with foreign DNA. The altered cell is then cloned into a plant.

The genetic engineering process creates massive collateral damage:

- Mutations are produced in hundreds or thousands of locations throughout the plant's DNA.
- Natural genes can be deleted or permanently turned on or off.
- Hundreds of genes may change their behavior.
- Even the inserted gene can be damaged or rearranged, and may create proteins that can trigger allergies or promote disease.

GM Foods on the Market

There are eight GM food crops. The five major varieties—soy, corn, canola, cotton, and sugar beets—have bacterial genes inserted, which allow the plants to survive an otherwise deadly dose of weed killer.

Farmers use considerably more herbicides on those GM crops and so the food has higher herbicide residues. About 68% of GM crops are herbicide tolerant.

FAST FACT

The cultivation and sale of genetically modified crops have been banned in Austria, France, Germany, Greece, Hungary, and Luxembourg.

The second GM trait is a built-in pesticide, found in GM corn and cotton. A gene from the soil bacterium called Bt (Bacillus thuringiensis) is inserted into the plant's DNA, where it secretes the insect-killing Bt-toxin in every cell. About 19% of GM crops produce their own pesticide. Another 13% produce a pesticide and are herbicide tolerant.

There is also GM Hawaiian papaya and a small amount of zucchini and yellow crookneck squash, which are engineered to resist a plant virus.

GM Foods and Allergies

GM soy and allergic reactions

- Soy allergies skyrocketed by 50% in the UK [United Kingdom], soon after GM soy was introduced.
- A skin prick allergy test shows that some people react to GM soy, but not to wild natural soy.

- Cooked GM soy contains as much as 7-times the amount of a known soy allergen.
- GM soy also contains a new unexpected allergen, not found in wild natural soy.

Bt corn and cotton linked to allergies
The biotech industry claims that Bt-toxin is harmless to humans and mammals because the natural bacteria version has been used as a spray by farmers for years. In reality, hundreds of people exposed to Bt spray had allergic-type symptoms, and mice fed Bt-toxin had powerful immune responses and damaged intestines. Moreover, the Bt in GM crops is designed to be more toxic than the natural spray and is thousands of times more concentrated.

Farm workers throughout India are getting the same allergic reactions from handling Bt cotton as those who reacted to Bt spray. Mice and rats fed Bt corn also showed immune responses.

German and French farmers protest the use of GM food in June 2005. Protests across Europe caused Austria, France, Germany, Greece, Hungary, and Luxembourg to ban GM crops.

GMOs fail allergy tests

No tests can guarantee that a GMO will not cause allergies. Although the World Health Organization recommends a screening protocol, the GM soy, corn, and papaya in our food supply fail those tests—because their GM proteins have properties of known allergens.

GMOs may make you allergic to non-GM foods

- GM soy drastically reduces digestive enzymes in mice. If it also impairs your digestion, you may become sensitive and allergic to a variety of foods.
- Mice fed Bt-toxin started having immune reactions to formerly harmless foods.
- Mice fed experimental GM peas also started reacting to a range of other foods. (The peas had already passed all the allergy tests normally done before a GMO gets on the market. Only this advanced test, which is never used on the GMOs we eat, revealed that the peas could actually be deadly.)

GM Foods and Health Problems

GMOs and liver problems

- Rats fed GM potatoes had smaller, partially atrophied livers.
- The livers of rats fed GM canola were 12–16% heavier.
- GM soy altered mouse liver cells in ways that suggest a toxic insult. The changes reversed after they switched to non-GM soy.

GMOs, reproductive problems, and infant mortality

- More than half the babies of mother rats fed GM soy died within three weeks.
- Male rats and mice fed GM soy had changed testicles, including altered young sperm cells in the mice.
- The DNA of mouse embryos functioned differently when their parents ate GM soy.
- The longer mice were fed GM corn, the less babies they had, and the smaller their babies were.

Bt crops linked to sterility, disease, and death

- Thousands of sheep, buffalo, and goats in India died after grazing on Bt cotton plants after harvest. Others suffered poor health and reproductive problems.

no i don't see any problems with genetically modified food

"No I don't see any problems with genetically modified food," cartoon by Wilbur-Dawbarn, www. CartoonStock.com.

- Farmers in Europe and Asia say that cows, water buffaloes, chickens, and horses died from eating Bt corn varieties.
- About two dozen US farmers report that Bt corn varieties caused widespread sterility in pigs or cows.
- Filipinos in at least five villages fell sick when a nearby Bt corn variety was pollinating.

The Need for Safety Evaluations

Unlike safety evaluations for drugs, there are no human clinical trials of GM foods. The only published human feeding experiment revealed that the genetic material inserted into GM soy transfers into bacteria living inside our intestines and continues to function. This means that long after we stop eating GM foods, we may still have their GM proteins produced continuously inside us.

- If the antibiotic gene inserted into most GM crops were to transfer, it could create super diseases, resistant to antibiotics.
- If the gene that creates Bt-toxin in GM corn were to transfer, it might turn our intestinal bacteria into living pesticide factories.
- Animal studies show that DNA in food can travel into organs throughout the body, even into the fetus.

In the 1980s, a contaminated brand of a food supplement called L-tryptophan killed about 100 Americans and caused sickness and disability in another 5,000–10,000 people. The source of contaminants was almost certainly the genetic engineering process used in its production. The disease took years to find and was almost overlooked. It was only identified because the symptoms were unique, acute, and fast-acting. If all three characteristics were not in place, the deadly GM supplement might never have been identified or removed.

If GM foods on the market are causing common diseases or if their effects appear only after long-term exposure, we may not be able to identify the source of the problem for decades, if at all. There is no monitoring of GMO-related illnesses and no long-term animal studies. Heavily invested biotech corporations are gambling with the health of our nation for their profit.

EVALUATING THE AUTHOR'S ARGUMENTS:

In this viewpoint the Institute for Responsible Technology uses the term *genetically modified* in reference to biotech crops. What might the Institute for Responsible Technology say about the use of the term *genetically enhanced* by John Reifsteck, the author of the previous viewpoint?

Viewpoint

3

Food Irradiation Is the Solution to Food-Borne Bacteria

Dennis T. Avery

"There is a solution, one that the newspapers and food-scare artists hate—electronic pasteurization."

In the following viewpoint Dennis T. Avery argues that the best way to eliminate food-borne bacteria is electronic pasteurization, or irradiation. Avery claims that the reaction to the 2010 salmonella-contaminated egg crisis has been to demand an increase in government regulation, which Avery claims is the wrong solution. He argues that bacteria such as salmonella are everywhere and more government regulation will not change this. Avery claims that the solution is to irradiate, or electronically pasteurize, all food, a treatment approved by the US Food and Drug Administration a decade ago for a variety of foods. Avery is the director of the Center for Global Food Issues at the Hudson Institute, where he edits *Global Food Quarterly*, and was formerly the senior agricultural analyst for the US Department of State.

Dennis T. Avery, "Why Tolerate Deadly Food Bacteria?" *American Daily*, October 4, 2010. Reproduced by permission.

AS YOU READ, CONSIDER THE FOLLOWING QUESTIONS:
1. According to the author, how many people were made ill by salmonella-contaminated eggs recently?
2. Salmonella kills about how many people a year, according to Avery?
3. Electronic pasteurization, or irradiation, has been approved for what four foods, according to the author?

We're into the second wave of anguish about the 1600 people made ill by salmonella-contaminated eggs, which caused the recall of a billion fresh eggs [in the summer of 2010].

Another Food Scare

"We're not in favor of government takeovers, but in the case of the egg producers who poisoned as many as 1,600 people with salmonella, we'll advocate that," said the *Frederick (MD) News-Post* on Oct 1st [2010].

"No one died, but the symptoms for some continue today—diarrhea, sickness, fever, not to mention the weeks of medical care needed by some victims, and the impact on other more conscientious egg producers in terms of lost sales. . . . This is an area where more government regulation is needed, and the free market cannot be relied on to govern itself," concludes the *News-Post*.

> **FAST FACT**
>
> Food irradiation—sometimes called cold pasteurization or electronic pasteurization—is the process of exposing food to ionizing radiation to destroy microorganisms, bacteria, viruses, and insects.

The food scare industry is rubbing its hands in glee. The public has been scared witless about its food safety again, the farmers are hanging their heads in shame—and the media response is to demand more expensive government regulation that won't kill the bacteria. Thus, the food scare industry can go right on flogging the food industry while people keep on getting sick.

And pretending this is all the fault of "industrial agriculture."

The Prevalence of Bacteria

I've got news, folks. Salmonella bacteria are pretty much everywhere, and always have been. Salmonella sickens more than a million people per year, according to the Centers for Disease Control, and kills about 400. The bacterium is found in ground beef, on lettuce, on spinach, even in peanut butter and unpasteurized orange juice. Salmonella can be inside the live chicken and even inside the eggs!

The even-more-dangerous E. coli: O157 is carried by cattle, and the U.S. Department of Agriculture says it has never tested for the bacterium in any cattle herd without finding it.

Remember that awful spinach O157 outbreak a couple of years ago with three deaths? There were cattle nearby. There were wild pigs running around through both the cattle pasture and the spinach field.

It's also true that the spinach field was in transition to organic production. That means the farmer couldn't use chemical fertilizers on it. Did he use composted cow manure? Are we sure that every bit of that composted cow manure got hot enough—130 to 150 degrees for 30 days—to kill the O157?

The University of California/Davis says they've found occasional O157 infections in wild pigs, coyotes, mice, crows, and cowbirds.

Irradiation destroys microorganisms on food and prolongs shelf life. The strawberries on the left were irradiated while the ones on the right were not.

US Opinion on Food Safety

Polling was conducted by telephone *February 17–18, 2009*, in the evenings. The total sample is 900 registered voters nationwide with a margin of error of plus or minus 3 percentage points.

In general, how concerned are you about the safety of the food that you eat?

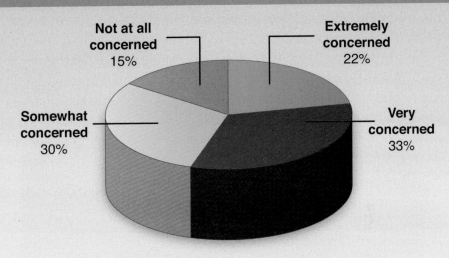

Not at all concerned 15%

Extremely concerned 22%

Somewhat concerned 30%

Very concerned 33%

Taken from: Fox News Poll by Opinion Dynamics, February 20, 2009.

How does more government regulation keep the food safe from all this natural risk?

The Food Irradiation Solution

There is a solution, one that the newspapers and food-scare artists hate—electronic pasteurization. Hitting the fresh food with an electron beam is cheap, quick, and kills virtually all of the food-borne bacteria on your food. It even kills the bacteria that promote rotting, so your fresh produce will taste even fresher.

The FDA [US Food and Drug Administration] approved electronic pasteurization for eggs ten years ago. The treatment has also been approved for poultry, fresh produce, and hamburger. But the food stores are frightened that news of electron beams will set off consumer boycotts—fear encouraged and managed by the food scare activists.

Think about the *News-Post*'s litany of suffering for 1,600 egg consumers—and multiply it by 875—to get the annual national illness impact of salmonella. Add 400 deaths. That doesn't even include the deaths and agony from O157. We in the United States have the safest food system the world has ever known. Don't let food-scare pushers tell you otherwise. It would take only this already-approved step to eliminate the bacteria that causes a million of us each year to suffer the misery of what we commonly call "food poisoning" and what, occasionally, causes death.

Isn't it time for consumer organizations to support electronic pasteurization? What can you do to protect your family? Start with talking to your grocery store manager about your support for electronic pasteurization.

> **EVALUATING THE AUTHOR'S ARGUMENTS:**
>
> In this viewpoint Dennis T. Avery uses the term *electronic pasteurization*, whereas Food & Water Watch, the author of the following viewpoint, uses *irradiation*. What do you think the significance is of these respective authors' using different terminology?

Irradiation Is Not a Good Solution to Food-Borne Illness

"Food producers need to address the source of the problem . . . not promote an expensive, impractical and ineffective technology like irradiation."

Food & Water Watch

In the following viewpoint Food & Water Watch argues that food irradiation is an expensive, ineffective, and impractical solution to food-borne illness. Food & Water Watch claims that extensive food irradiation would require many costly irradiation facilities that would make food more expensive. In addition, the author claims that irradiation is not completely effective but nonetheless would encourage food producers to take less caution, increasing the risk of food-borne illness. Food & Water Watch says that irradiation is impractical since it destroys vital nutrients and may also be dangerous for consumers. Food & Water Watch is a nonprofit organization that advocates for policies that will result in safe food and affordable drinking water.

AS YOU READ, CONSIDER THE FOLLOWING QUESTIONS:
1. Food & Water Watch claims that the US Food and Drug Administration first legalized what irradiated food in 1963?
2. How many multimillion-dollar facilities would be needed just to irradiate all the hamburger meat in America each year, according to the author?
3. The author says that irradiation would destroy up to what percentage of vitamin A in eggs?

D espite years of promotion from both industry and regulators, Americans have expressed their dislike and distrust of irradiated foods for more than 40 years, since FDA [US Food and Drug Administration] first legalized irradiated wheat in 1963. Numerous test-marketing efforts have failed, including irradiated ground beef from 2000 to 2004 and various irradiated fruits in the late 1980s and early 1990s.

The Food Irradiation Issue

Despite the argument by proponents that the safety of irradiation has been studied for over fifty years, many questions still remain about the long-term health effects of consuming a steady diet of irradiated foods. There are no studies to show that, over the long-term, eating irradiated foods is safe. Add in the nutritional damage irradiation can do to some foods and we believe it is far too soon to allow large portions of the food supply to be irradiated.

So far, Americans have eaten very little irradiated food. But in addition to eliminating the irradiation label, FDA is considering allowing irradiation of ready-to-eat foods such as hot dogs, deli meats, and bagged salads—a category of foods that make up a significant percentage of many people's diets.

The Food and Drug Administration is considering a rule change that would deprive consumers of accurate information about irradiation. Their proposal to change the rules for labeling irradiated food would allow it to be labeled as "pasteurized" in some cases, and in other cases to be sold without any labeling at all. With this proposal, the agency is ignoring overwhelming public input in support of clear and mandatory labeling of irradiated foods.

That 5,000 people in the United States die every year from food-borne illnesses is tragic. Food producers need to address the source of the problem—too-fast processing lines, too-long distances for food to travel, and dirty conditions at plants—not promote an expensive, impractical and ineffective technology like irradiation.

Irradiation Is Expensive and Ineffective

Irradiating the U.S. food supply would be extraordinarily expensive. In order to effectively irradiate the 8 billion pounds of hamburger that Americans eat every year, we would have to build approximately 80 multimillion dollar irradiation facilities. Further, irradiating the entire

The radura is the international symbol for irradiated food.

U.S. food supply would mean building thousands of plants. The costs of these facilities and the costs of transporting and handling irradiated food would be passed on to consumers. While the U.S. Department of Agriculture [USDA] has estimated that irradiated ground beef should cost an additional 13 cents to 20 cents per pound, surveys of supermarkets reveal an additional cost of 50 cents to one dollar per pound for irradiated ground beef products.

Irradiation does not kill all the bacteria in food and may undermine other food safety efforts by masking filthy conditions and encouraging improper handling. In 2007, Food & Water Watch complained to the USDA that Wegmans supermarkets improperly encouraged consumers to undercook irradiated meat in their "Some Like It Pink" press release.

"While irradiation may reduce the numbers of bacteria present in raw product, the technology does not necessarily render it commercially sterile. . . . Therefore, FSIS [USDA Food Safety and Inspection Service] advises consumers that all raw ground beef, including raw ground beef that has been irradiated, should be cooked to a minimum of 160 degrees Fahrenheit," wrote the USDA Food Safety and Inspection Services in a letter about Wegmans to Food & Water Watch.

Irradiation can be used to obscure poor sanitation in today's mega-sized livestock slaughterhouses and food processing plants. Slaughterhouses process up to 400 cows per hour or 200 birds per minute, posing an enormous sanitation challenge where *E. coli*, *Salmonella* and other potentially deadly food-borne pathogens can be spread through feces, urine and pus. Instead of encouraging expensive treatments like irradiation, USDA should give meat inspectors the tools to test products at the plant and ensure that contaminated meat never reaches restaurants or supermarket shelves.

Infected manure from a nearby beef cattle ranch was blamed for the *E. coli* spinach outbreak in California. In response, testing of water

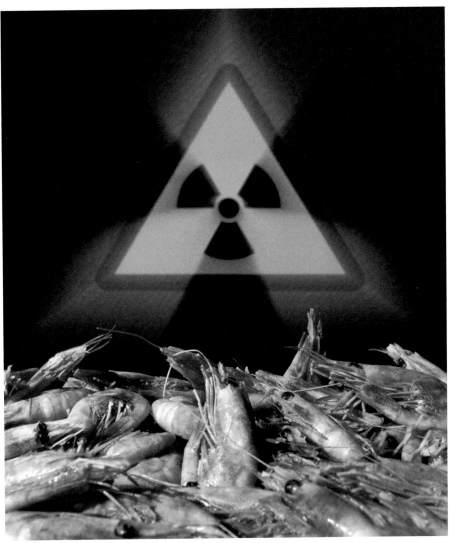

Food & Water Watch says that irradiation destroys vital nutrients and may also endanger consumers.

used for irrigation and washing should be improved, vegetable processing plants should be inspected more thoroughly, large livestock operations operating near cropland should be more tightly regulated, and employees processing vegetable[s] should be better trained.

Irradiation Is Impractical and May Be Dangerous

Irradiation damages many foods and can ruin their flavor, odor, and texture. The process destroys vitamins, protein, essential fatty acids and other nutrients—up to 80 percent of vitamin A in eggs and half the beta carotene in orange juice. A dose of radiation sufficient to kill bacteria in fragile produce such as spinach would render it inedible.

Today, there are only two operating commercial irradiation facilities, located in Iowa and Florida, specifically designed to irradiate food. Finding hubs for irradiation facilities to treat vegetables produced by farms all over the country would be difficult. And fresh lettuce, spinach and other vegetables have a very short shelf-life, so they very likely could not survive the additional transportation and handling time that irradiation requires.

The U.S. Food & Drug Administration approved food irradiation for many foods in spite of paltry and flawed data on safety and in violation of their own safety protocols. However, between the cost, the practical problems, and consumer distaste for the technology, very little irradiated food is on supermarket shelves today. A push to irradiate a significant portion of the U.S. food supply would effectively subject the American public to a huge experiment on the safety of irradiated foods, [Food & Water Watch director Wenonah] Hauter said.

Scientists have observed serious health problems in lab animals fed irradiated foods. Those include premature death, cancer, tumors, stillbirths, mutations, organ damage, immune system failure and stunted growth. In one experiment, genetic damage was detected in young children who ate irradiated wheat. In some foods, irradiation forms chemicals known or suspected to cause cancer and birth defects. One chemical, 2-ACBs, has been linked to cancer development in rats and genetic damage in human cells.

EVALUATING THE AUTHOR'S ARGUMENTS:

In this viewpoint Food & Water Watch worries that extensive food irradiation would cause food producers to become more lax in their handling of food. What do you think that Dennis T. Avery, the author of the previous viewpoint, would say in response to this concern?

Viewpoint 5

Scientific Evidence Has Not Shown That Genetically Modified Salmon Is Safe

Alexis Baden-Mayer

"The data does not show that [genetically engineered] salmon is similar enough to normal salmon to be considered safe."

In the following viewpoint Alexis Baden-Mayer argues that there is not enough evidence for the US Food and Drug Administration to approve genetically engineered (GE) salmon for human consumption. Baden-Mayer contends that there is not enough research on GE salmon DNA to assume that it is safe. She criticizes the data put forth by the biotechnology company AquaBounty in support of GE salmon, claiming that flaws and biases in the data do not support the conclusion that GE salmon is similar to normal salmon. Furthermore, Baden-Mayer claims that the data itself show worrisome differences between GE salmon and normal salmon that ought to keep GE salmon out of the food supply. Baden-Mayer is the political director of the Organic Consumers Association, a public interest organization campaigning for health, justice, and sustainability.

AS YOU READ, CONSIDER THE FOLLOWING QUESTIONS:
1. The author claims that since 1992 the US Food and Drug Administration has operated under what legal fiction?
2. For what reason does the author believe the food safety data for genetically engineered salmon provided by AquaBounty may have been biased?
3. Baden-Mayer claims that genetically engineered salmon have mean allergenic potencies that are how much higher than normal salmon?

G E [genetically engineered] salmon should not be approved for human consumption based on the data FDA [US Food and Drug Administration] has collected from [biotechnology company] AquaBounty. The data does not show that GE salmon is similar enough to normal salmon to be considered safe.

The Food Safety Data on GE Salmon DNA
The FDA's policy of using the process for animal drugs to review GE animals is entirely inappropriate and needs to be replaced before people start eating genetically engineered animals.

But, putting that issue aside, OCA [Organic Consumers Association] has a number of concerns about the accuracy and interpretation of the data FDA used as the basis for its decision that GE salmon is safe to eat.

First, it is important to note that the FDA did not require food safety data on genetically engineered salmon DNA.

The human health impacts of consuming the "AquaBounty construct" are unknown and are not being investigated. Since 1992, the FDA has operated under the legal fiction that there is no risk associated with the human consumption of genetically engineered DNA. As the FDA explains, under this policy, because DNA is

Generally Recognized as Safe, engineered DNA is considered safe, as well.

I'd like to call your attention to a human study conducted by the UK's [United Kingdom's] Food Standards Agency that found that a single meal of genetically engineered soy can result in "horizontal gene transfer," where the bacteria of the gut takes up the soy's modified DNA. Research must be done to determine whether this would happen to people who eat AquAdvantage Salmon and what the health implications would be.

In September 2010 the Food and Drug Administration held public hearings on whether to approve genetically modified salmon. At the hearings, a Food & Water Watch member presents a box of public comments that oppose the proposal.

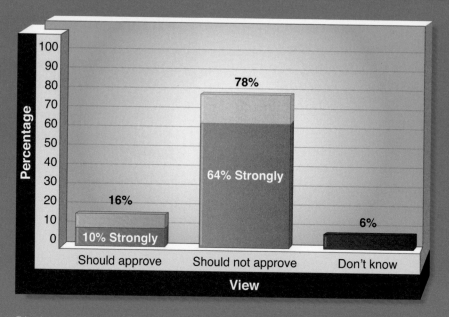

Views on FDA Approval of Genetically Engineered Salmon

- 78% — Should not approve (64% Strongly)
- 16% — Should approve (10% Strongly)
- 6% — Don't know

Percentage / View

Taken from: Lake Research Partners telephone survey conducted among a national probability sample of 1,000 adults 18 years of age and older, September 9–12, 2010.

A Flawed Study

Instead of researching the safety of consuming GE salmon DNA, the FDA food safety review was a simple quacks-like-a-duck-style comparison of GE and normal salmon for hormone levels, nutrition and allergenic potency. Even using this elementary analysis, the data used to support the FDA's conclusion that GE salmon is similar enough to normal salmon to be considered safe is seriously flawed.

1. The FDA didn't always segregate and sometimes didn't even collect data from AquaBounty on the actual fish that people will be eating, the Panama-raised triploid, monosex AquAdvantage Salmon. Instead, each of the food safety studies look at genetically engineered salmon, in general.

2. The FDA did not require AquaBounty to show that GE salmon is the same as normal salmon when raised under the same conditions. In addition to AquaBounty's control salmon, the FDA compared GE

salmon to farmed salmon raised under unknown conditions and data from other salmon studies.

3. AquaBounty tested only a few fish, making it less likely that its food safety studies would reveal statistically significant differences between genetically engineered and normal salmon.

4. AquaBounty's detection levels were sometimes too low to produce food safety data for comparison.

5. AquaBounty selected which fish to test and unblinded samples, which may have biased the food safety data.

The Differences Between GE and Normal Salmon

Even with all the flaws and biases that are likely to have hidden some of the differences, the data showed that genetically engineered and normal salmon do not have the same hormone levels, nutrition or allergenic potency.

GE salmon has 40% more IGF1, a hormone linked to prostate, breast and colon cancers in humans.

GE salmon is less nutritious than normal salmon. It has the lowest omega-3 to omega-6 ratio of all the salmon in the studies FDA reviewed.

GE salmon have mean allergenic potencies that are 20% and 52% higher than normal salmon, increasing the risk of potentially deadly allergic reactions.

With all that we know and all that we know we do not know about GE salmon, there is no other way to protect public health than to keep it out of the food supply.

EVALUATING THE AUTHOR'S ARGUMENTS:

In this viewpoint Alexis Baden-Mayer says that genetically engineered salmon must be kept out of the food supply partially because of what we do not know. What other author(s) in this chapter take this approach to food safety?

Scientific Evidence Has Not Shown That Genetically Modified Salmon Is Unsafe

Jon Entine

"[Genetically modified] food . . . faces resistance from people who . . . worry about risks that while minimal are hard to understand, invisible and undetectable."

In the following viewpoint Jon Entine argues that objections to genetically modified (GM) salmon are unfounded. Entine claims that objections to GM salmon are coming from both the far right and the left, and that both are mistaken. He claims that it is irrational fear of science and distrust of government that is driving the resistance to genetically modified organisms in general and GM salmon in particular. Entine concludes that GM salmon is essentially identical to natural salmon and that resistance to it is driven by an irrational psychology and not by science. Entine is a journalist, think tank scholar, and organizational consultant. He is the author of *Let Them Eat*

Precaution: How Politics Is Undermining the Genetic Revolution in Agriculture.

AS YOU READ, CONSIDER THE FOLLOWING QUESTIONS:
1. What are three examples the author gives of the second generation of genetically modified foods?
2. According to Entine, what two precautions will be taken so that genetically modified salmon do not interbreed with wild fish?
3. What percentage of scientists identify as conservative, according to the author?

News that the US Food and Drug Administration [FDA] is about to bless the sale of the first genetically modified [GM] food—salmon—set off the familiar outcry among anti-GM activists.

By all reports, the Massachusetts firm AquaBounty will get the OK this autumn [2010—in June 2011, Congress banned FDA's approving of the GM fish] to sell salmon eggs programmed to produce a full-grown Atlantic salmon in about half the time it currently takes on a farm. It took a gene from one species that matures faster, the Chinook, and another gene from the ocean pout, a distant cousin of salmon, that switches on the Chinook growth gene.

FAST FACT

AquaBounty, the biotechnology company that developed genetically modified (GM) eggs for AquAdvantage Salmon, opposes labeling of GM salmon because it says it is "nutritionally and biologically the same as any other Atlantic salmon."

The Anti-GM Establishment

The naturalistic religious left then kicked into gear. Headlines decrying "FrankenSalmon" sprouted. Food & Water Watch, which has no scientists on its staff, launched a protest based on the claim that government doesn't have the expertise to evaluate the impact of GM on human health and the environment. Most disturbingly, its position is backed by groups such as the

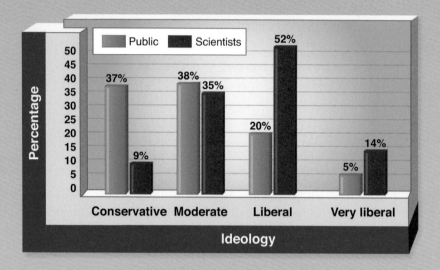

Partisanship and Ideology in the Public and Among Scientists

Legend: Public | Scientists

Percentage (y-axis): 0, 5, 10, 15, 20, 25, 30, 35, 40, 45, 50

- Conservative: Public 37%, Scientists 9%
- Moderate: Public 38%, Scientists 35%
- Liberal: Public 20%, Scientists 52%
- Very liberal: Public 5%, Scientists 14%

Ideology (x-axis)

Taken from: Pew Research Center for the People and the Press, "Public Praises Science; Scientists Fault Public, Media," July 9, 2009.

Council for Responsible Genetics in the US and GeneWatch in the UK [United Kingdom].

Most recently, the US Supreme Court rejected a suit filed by the Centre for Food Safety (CFS) to block the introduction of bioengineered alfalfa. After an exhaustive review in 2005, the US Department of Agriculture gave the alfalfa—modified to tolerate glyphosate, a herbicide produced by Monsanto commercially known as Roundup—the green light. CFS successfully sued, requiring the department to revisit its ruling. A draft of that second evaluation, released in December 2009, echoed the original findings, which should lead soon to clearance of the GM alfalfa sales [USDA gave its ok in January 2011].

A sizable anti-GM establishment is behind almost every campaign to gut the introduction of bioengineering, especially in the agricultural sector, where the technology has been successfully used for decades.

Significant proportions of soybean (77% of global harvest), maize (26% of feed) and canola (21%) crops engineered to be grown with less use of insecticides have been part of the world diet for years with no negative consequences.

All told, 60 to 70 transgenic crops have been developed. Now we're moving into the second generation of GM foods: ones modified with special qualities such as faster growth (salmon), greater nutrition (aubergine [eggplant] and rice), or the ability to cut pollution from waste (pigs).

Objections on the Right and Left

Fear of science and mistrust of government oversight brings together the worst impulses of the far right and the loony left. Religious conservatives have long opposed stem cell research as manipulating God's way. Substitute "nature" for "God" and roll out such sober-sounding phrases as "unintended consequences" and you have the left's limp justification for its anti-GM hegemony.

Both groups' suspicions extend to medicine, where bioengineering's benefits are undeniable. Gene therapy can help treat immune deficiencies. It's used to create GM bacteria and rodents that are essential tools of modern research. Biotechnology has been successful

Genetically modified salmon grow in tanks at a fish farm in Massachusetts. The company, AquaBounty, says the salmon are no different than any other Atlantic salmon.

in mass-producing insulin, human growth hormones, follistim for treating infertility, vaccines . . . the list goes on and on.

What's most disturbing is that anti-GM hysteria is now part of the mainstream left, which embraces naturalism almost as religion, with the precautionary principle (selectively applied) as its central canon.

The loudest objections to the GM salmon are that we are "messing with nature." But this fish is 100% salmon and to avoid interbreeding with wild fish, females are grown sterile and GM salmon are only sold to companies that will breed them in inland tanks.

Science and Psychology

The left's squeamishness is odd because scientists are overwhelmingly liberal. A Pew Research Centre study found that only 9% of scientists viewed themselves as conservative while 52% say they are liberal or very liberal.

So, while scientists, mostly leftists, focus on how to harness the future, activist groups aggressively scare the public, often intimidating legislators. Psychology, not science, drives the resistance. GM food that is essentially identical to the natural kind, which offers the promise of more sustainable production of more protein at less cost faces resistance from people who, as we all do to some degree, worry about risks that while minimal are hard to understand, invisible and undetectable. Like the far right, they do not trust government bureaucracy to protect us.

The bottom line is: anti-science extremists on the left and right can't handle the truth.

> **EVALUATING THE AUTHOR'S ARGUMENTS:**
>
> In this viewpoint Jon Entine rejects the objection to genetically modified salmon on the basis of its being unnatural. Is naturalness a relevant concern when it comes to food safety? Give one reason for and one reason against the view that tinkering with nature should be avoided when it comes to food.

Chapter 3

Are Certain Foods Unsafe to Eat?

The US Department of Agriculture does not require US meat producers to test for mad cow disease. The policy has caused worldwide controversy.

All US Beef Needs to Be Tested for Mad Cow Disease to Ensure Safety

Jim Hightower

"'Eat it and shut up' seems to be America's marketing slogan."

In the following viewpoint Jim Hightower argues that the United States should begin testing all cows that go to slaughter for mad cow disease. Hightower contends that Americans should be more like the South Korean people, who protested the lift of a ban on US beef, and demand that cows be tested. Hightower claims that there is an inexpensive and simple test to check for mad cow disease, and he laments that it is not even allowed by private companies. He points to the fact that the vast majority of Americans would be willing to pay the increased cost for tested beef. Hightower wonders if the US resistance to mad cow testing might mask a fear that mad cow disease is much more prevalent than is thought. Hightower is coeditor and cofounder of the newsletter *Hightower Lowdown* and the author of *Swim Against the Current: Even a Dead Fish Can Go with the Flow.*

Jim Hightower, "Legitimate Beef," *Progressive*, September 2008, vol. 72, no. 9, p. 46. This piece was originally written for *The Progressive* magazine, 409 E. Main St., Madison, WI 53703. www.progressivemediaproject.org.

What is it with those kooky South Koreans? Tens of thousands of them rushed into the streets to protest—get this—beef. Specifically, beef imported from the United States. Are they nuts? Or, do they know something we don't?

Mad Cow Disease from America

South Koreans are rejecting our steaks and burgers because of the widespread belief there that America's industrialized production process brings a deadly dose of Mad Cow disease to the plate. Once the third largest importer of U.S. beef, South Korea shut its ports to our product after the brain-wasting livestock disease was confirmed in America in 2003. This April [2008], however, President Lee Myung-bak gave in to industry pressure and issued an edict that lifted his country's ban.

Bad move. Consumers, furious that he would sell out their nation's health to global trade hucksters, exploded all over Lee,

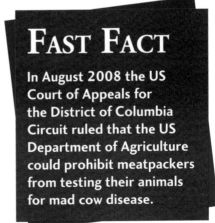

FAST FACT

In August 2008 the US Court of Appeals for the District of Columbia Circuit ruled that the US Department of Agriculture could prohibit meatpackers from testing their animals for mad cow disease.

who became the first Korean president brought to his knees by steak. He was forced to apologize for his mishandling of the issue, he fired all but one of his top aides, the entire cabinet submitted

US Meat and Livestock Trade, 2002–2008

Top markets for US beef*
(accounting for over 90 percent of total beef exports)

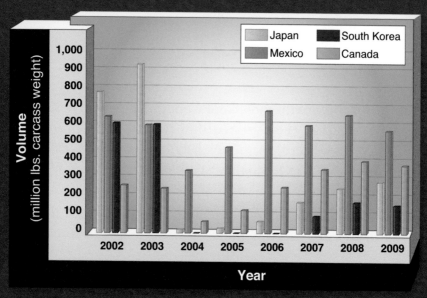

*Note: Total beef exports to South Korea and Japan include several processed meat categories, each of which is assumed to contain a specific portion of beef.

Taken from: USDA Economic Research Service, "U.S. Beef and Cattle Industry: Background Statistics and Information," July 10, 2010.

their resignations, and he hastily renegotiated a trimmed deal with American officials.

Still, the protests continued, with insistent demands for Lee's hide, and he resorted to a heavy-handed police crackdown. Despite allowing a small amount of U.S. beef into the country, major supermarkets and restaurants refuse to sell it, and even McDonald's stresses in its ads that its Korean franchises make their burgers with Australian beef. When Condoleezza Rice made a June diplomatic visit to Seoul, she was greeted with protest placards demanding, "Stop Rice and Mad Cow."

The Testing Solution

The official American response is to depict South Koreans as silly consumers, scared of a bugaboo in their burgers. But is it a bugaboo?

The ones being silly are our own ag officials and corporate beef purveyors. They could easily assure our Korean customers that the beef we ship to them is free of Mad Cow disease by conducting a test on each cow as it goes to slaughter. Called rapid test, this cheap, simple, reliable screening can detect the disease even in animals that do not yet show any "mad" symptoms, giving slaughter-houses the ability to prevent all tainted cows from entering the food supply. Europe and Japan already do this, thus assuring their foreign customers that their beef does not carry the disease.

The Bush agriculture department, however, refuses to implement such a system or even to let private companies use the rapid test on their own as a way of meeting their customers' demand for mad-free meat. Instead, the department and the giant meat exporters it serves

South Koreans protest against the importation of American beef because it is not tested for mad cow disease.

arrogantly insist that the world must simply trust that every ounce of America's beef is pure because we say it is.

"I want to assure everyone that American beef is safe," Rice announced in Seoul, as though her word should be enough. "Eat it and shut up" seems to be America's marketing slogan.

Support for Mad Cow Testing

Meanwhile, back at the home place, a Consumers Union survey found that 71 percent of American beef eaters are willing to pay up to a dime more per pound to cover the cost of Mad Cow testing on all of our domestic beef supply. So, why is USDA [US Department of Agriculture] so boneheaded? One reason is that testing most likely would reveal that the American industry has a much larger Mad Cow problem than it's been willing to admit. In Europe, for example, a pilot testing program turned up not a few cases, but 1,117 cows that carried the disease, even though they showed no symptoms and had been cleared to enter the food supply.

It's not Korean consumers who are crazy—it's our own public officials.

EVALUATING THE AUTHOR'S ARGUMENTS:

In this viewpoint Jim Hightower argues for mad cow testing for all US cattle. Name at least one feature of the test highlighted by Hightower that is contradicted by the American Meat Institute, the author of the following viewpoint.

Viewpoint

2

Testing All US Beef for Mad Cow Disease Is a Waste of Resources

American Meat Institute

"Testing all cattle for BSE doesn't make scientific or practical sense."

In the following viewpoint the American Meat Institute argues that testing all cattle for mad cow disease is pointless. The author claims that most of the cattle slaughtered for beef in the United States are too young to have developed mad cow disease. The American Meat Institute claims that the best way to ensure US beef is free of mad cow disease is to adhere to the US Food and Drug Administration guidelines for prevention, which include selective testing of at-risk cattle and removal of potentially infective materials. Testing all cattle, the American Meat Institute concludes, would be a waste of resources that could be spent in more productive ways to ensure the safety of US beef. The American Meat Institute is a national trade association that represents packers and processors of meat and poultry products and their suppliers.

AS YOU READ, CONSIDER THE FOLLOWING QUESTIONS:
1. The American Meat Institute draws an analogy between testing young cattle for mad cow disease and testing young children for what?
2. What percentage of cattle slaughtered in the United States, according to the author, are under thirty months of age?
3. The American Meat Institute claims that each test for mad cow disease would cost about how much just for the test kits?

M uch discussion has occurred about the value of testing 100 percent of cattle for BSE [bovine spongiform encephalopathy, or mad cow disease]. While testing certain subpopulations of cattle is useful in surveillance of animal diseases, testing all cattle for BSE doesn't make scientific or practical sense. Why? BSE occurs in older cattle and the vast majority of U.S. cattle are processed years before BSE could ever be detected.

Selective Testing

While testing young animals may sound reassuring, such a costly but ineffective endeavor is much like testing young children for Alzheimer's Disease. Targeting the testing towards older, higher risk cattle populations is the most effective strategy. The most important fact to remember is that beef has never been associated with a BSE-related illness, regardless of its country of origin or the age of the animal.

Targeted surveillance testing of cattle for BSE is one of the firewalls the U.S. Department of Agriculture has deployed to monitor the effectiveness of its BSE prevention strategies. The U.S. Department of Agriculture administers tests to animals that 1) show symptoms of a neurological disorder, 2) are non-ambulatory, which could indicate a potential illness

FAST FACT

The US Department of Agriculture's Animal and Plant Health Inspection Service has conducted surveillance for mad cow disease since 1990.

or 3) are old enough to have developed the disease (greater than 30 months of age).

The U.S. system will detect BSE with a high degree of certainty if it is present in U.S. herds. This is a scientifically based approach. It makes no sense to test a category of cattle that will always test negative.

The Limits of BSE Testing

Animals that develop BSE typically are exposed through contaminated feed, at a young age. Strict regulations are in place in the United

A researcher performs a mad cow disease test using a small sample of cow brain. The American Meat Institute says testing all cattle is pointless because US cows are slaughtered too young to have contracted the disease.

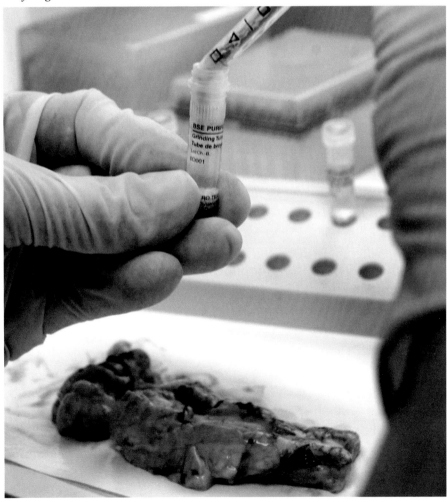

The Science of BSE Testing

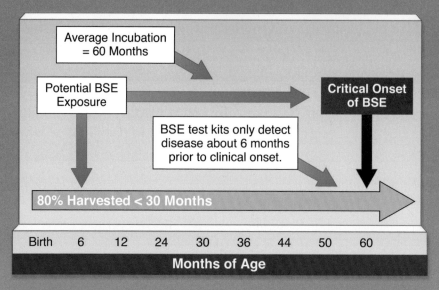

Taken from: "BSE: Testing – What It Can and Cannot Accomplish," American Meat Institute Fact Sheet, June 2009.

States to prevent such contamination and compliance is at nearly 100 percent, according to the U.S. Department of Agriculture.

The disease cannot be detected in infected animals until they are of advanced age when the infective agent begins to accumulate in the brain and neurological tissues—tissues that are removed from cattle and do not enter the food supply.

The majority of cattle (over 80 percent) slaughtered in the United States are under 30 months of age. . . .

The test is only able to detect the disease three to six months prior to clinical onset. When you couple these technical limitations with the fact that BSE occurs in cattle that are nearly three times the median age of those processed in the United States, it becomes clear that testing young cattle is scientifically indefensible. As Dr. Will Hueston, a veterinarian and member of the International BSE Review Teams for both Canada and United States recently stated, ". . . recommending the testing of young animals [for BSE] would be veterinary malpractice—and is no different than human doctors billing Medicare for unneeded tests and procedures."

The Most Effective Method

Scientists and public health experts agree that the most effective method for protecting the public health is removing potentially infective materials—the so-called "specified risk materials (SRMs)." This is done effectively in the United States with continuous oversight from federal inspectors, who are in packing plants during every minute of operation. By law all cattle destined for human consumption must have the SRMs removed.

According to rules governed by the World Organization for Animal Health (OIE), all countries that have had a case of BSE must remove cattle SRMs before beef can be exported to other countries.

Cost is a major issue: Each test would cost about $20–$30 for the test kits alone. Costs would likely more than double once labor and shipping are included. Swiss government officials have estimated their cost is $60 per head. It is likely that universal, mandatory testing of all cattle slaughtered in the United States would cost in excess of more than $1 billion per year. This cost would be borne by both the industry and consumers.

Testing is a valuable tool that allows the federal government to monitor the health of the U.S. herd and gauge the success of our strategies for preventing BSE. Since June 2004, nearly one million animals have been tested as part of USDA's surveillance program, which exceeds international animal health guidelines.

One hundred percent testing of all cattle for BSE is a waste of resources that could be better spent where they can truly have a public impact. Because BSE occurs in older cattle, some experts have said that such testing is actually misleading to consumers. The results will always be negative and provide no added food safety assurance.

EVALUATING THE AUTHOR'S ARGUMENTS:

In this viewpoint the American Meat Institute claims that the test for mad cow disease is too expensive. What statistic might Jim Hightower, the author of the preceding viewpoint, raise in response to this?

High Fructose Corn Syrup Is Unsafe in Any Amount

"High fructose corn syrup is not natural, it is genetically modified and it does not offer the body any nutritional benefits."

Jennifer Kelly

In the following viewpoint Jennifer Kelly argues that high fructose corn syrup (HFCS) is not safe to eat. Kelly claims that the recent advertising campaign by the Corn Refiners Association is misleading. She claims that HFCS is neither natural nor fine in moderation. She claims that comparing HFCS to sugar is no help either, as refined sugar is not healthy. Kelly claims that the motive of the Corn Refiners Association in promoting HFCS is an interest in profit. She concludes that people would be better off completely avoiding HFCS and only consuming natural, unrefined sweeteners. Kelly is a board-certified holistic health practitioner in New York State.

AS YOU READ, CONSIDER THE FOLLOWING QUESTIONS:
1. Kelly argues that high fructose corn syrup is highly foreign to the human digestive and nervous systems because of what?
2. The author claims that high fructose corn syrup metabolizes into fat more rapidly than sugar, especially when consumed in what form?
3. What five sweeteners does Kelly claim are unrefined and provide the body with nutrients?

I n a recent television commercial sponsored by the Corn Refiners Association [CRA], one concerned mom is made to look the fool when she fails to respond as to why she should avoid giving her children high fructose corn syrup [HFCS]. She, like many of us, has heard that the seemingly omnipresent sweetener is unhealthy. She's absolutely correct.

The HFCS Advertising Campaign

The multimillion-dollar advertising campaign launched by the CRA is a result of growing awareness of the dangers of HFCS and the desire to keep concerned health-seekers in the dark about the truth. Unlike the stunned mom in the commercial, readers of this editorial will be armed with a clear response when confronted with HFCS proponents.

The website accompanying the CRA's television ad series, www.sweetsurprise.com, claims that HFCS is natural because it is made from corn. By that logic, consuming ethanol, also made from corn, should be as safe as sugar and "fine in moderation." The fact is, however, that there is nothing natural about HFCS—there is no tree or plant producing it; it does not sprout from the earth. HFCS is the result of a complicated manufacturing process which breaks down cornstarch and treats it with three different enzymes, two of which are genetically modified organisms [GMOs], according to Linda Forristal, in a 2001 article appearing in the *Weston Price Foundation* quarterly magazine. In addition to the GMO enzymes used, the majority of corn in the United States is also genetically modified, thereby yielding a product (HFCS) highly foreign to the human digestive and nervous systems.

FAST FACT

The Corn Refiners Association has petitioned the US Food and Drug Administration to allow the term *corn sugar* as an alternative label declaration for high fructose corn syrup.

The Similarity to Sugar

The CRA claims HFCS is nutritionally the same as sugar, yet the man-made substance does not metabolize in the body the same way

Obesity and High Fructose Corn Syrup

The number of Americans who are obese has quadrupled in recent years, a study shows. At the same time, high fructose corn syrup consumption has risen at parallel rates.

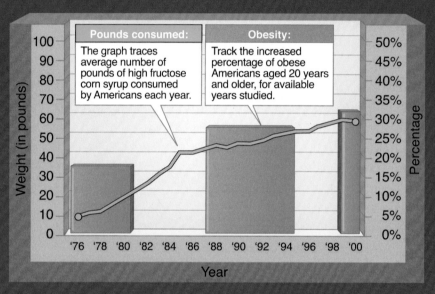

Pounds consumed: The graph traces average number of pounds of high fructose corn syrup consumed by Americans each year.

Obesity: Track the increased percentage of obese Americans aged 20 years and older, for available years studied.

Original Source: Centers for Disease Control and Prevention, American Obesity Association, Chronicle Research.

Taken from: Kim Severson, "Sugar Coated / We're Drowning in High Fructose Corn Syrup. Do the Risks Go Beyond Our Waistline?," *San Francisco Chronicle*, February 18, 2004.

table sugar (sucrose) does. The main difference between the two is that HFCS contains unbound fructose (which, among other concerns, has been found to interfere with the heart's use of key minerals) and glucose molecules, while sucrose is a larger molecule that metabolizes into glucose and fructose. According to research by renowned food expert Dr. Joseph Mercola, as well as by Dr. Meira Fields at the USDA [US Department of Agriculture], HFCS metabolizes into fat more rapidly than any other sugar, especially when consumed in liquid form, such as in sodas, soft drinks and juices.

The idea that HFCS is fine "in moderation" is also problematic. Other than the belief that consumption of GMOs in any amount is unsafe (evidence of the dangers of GMOs is well documented), there is the undeniable reality that HFCS is difficult to avoid, as it appears in a vast multitude of foods and beverages, from bread and cereals to ketchup and cough syrups. Indeed, it is an arduous task to consume HFCS only in moderation. The startling fact that HFCS is the #1 source of calories in the United States speaks to the virtual assault on Americans that has been taking place over the last 20 years.

In any regard, to claim HFCS is as safe as sugar is not exactly high praise for the processed sweetener. Refined table sugar is not healthy, either. What else would have caused the need for the development of so many artificial sweeteners, but for the detriments of sugar? Substances that have been processed and stripped of the nutrients they started with are thereby depleted of enzymes that could have been used to assist in digestion. Without these vital catalysts from food, the body is forced to use its own, limited store of enzymes. Processed foods including either refined sugars or HFCS are, therefore, truly empty calories, as they provide the body with little or none of the nutrition it requires.

Many food and beverage companies, such as Pepsi, have gone back to using cane sugar instead of high fructose corn syrup in some of their products.

The Nutritional Benefits of Natural Sweeteners

The need for sweetness can be met through natural sweeteners with real ingredients that come from nature's perfect recipes for exactly what the human body craves. Unrefined sugar cane and sweeteners like agave nectar, yacon root syrup, honey and maple syrup can substitute for the refined sugars and provide the body with nutrients along the way.

If HFCS were not inexpensive and profitable for its manufacturers, the CRA would not be spending millions to promote the very unnatural sweetener, which has become a staple of the American diet. There is no real concern for the health of the American public behind the HFCS campaign; its sole motivation is profit.

The retort, then, when confronted with advocates of the cheap, ubiquitous sweetener, is simple: high fructose corn syrup is not natural, it is genetically modified and it does not offer the body any nutritional benefits; on the contrary, it robs enzymes and turns quickly to fat.

There are no controversies surrounding foods that the earth provides; there is no debate over whether or not fruits, vegetables, seeds, nuts and herbs are "natural." Nature holds everything the body requires. Maybe in returning to simpler, more basic sources of nutrition, Americans can finally find the sweetness they have been missing.

EVALUATING THE AUTHOR'S ARGUMENTS:

In this viewpoint Jennifer Kelly claims that high fructose corn syrup is not natural just because it is made from corn, arguing that ethanol—which is made from corn—is not safe to eat. Does her logic succeed in showing why high fructose corn syrup is not natural? Why or why not?

Viewpoint

4

There Is No Evidence That High Fructose Corn Syrup Is Unsafe

J. Justin Wilson

"High fructose corn syrup, despite all the media hype, is nutritionally the same as the table sugar that people add to their coffee."

In the following viewpoint J. Justin Wilson contends that high fructose corn syrup (HFCS) is just as safe as sugar, despite hype to the contrary. Wilson claims that HFCS and sugar are nearly identical in every way, and both are composed of fructose and glucose. Wilson claims that there have been some misleading studies that have confused consumers, causing them to believe that HFCS is unhealthy. On the contrary, Wilson claims, HFCS has been found to be natural and safe. Wilson concludes that the move away from HFCS is a fad unfounded on science. Wilson is the senior research analyst at the Center for Consumer Freedom, a nonprofit coalition that works to promote personal responsibility and protect consumer choices.

AS YOU READ, CONSIDER THE FOLLOWING QUESTIONS:
1. According to Wilson, high fructose corn syrup (HFCS) is composed of fructose in what amount?
2. The US Food and Drug Administration has put HFCS in what category of ingredients, according to the author?
3. What two items does Wilson warn might be the subject of the next "bad" food campaign based on a fad diet myth?

S tarbucks announced that it will make a major change in its baked goods by the end of the month [June 2009], removing high fructose corn syrup [HFCS] as part of a switch to "real" food. But before you gag on your blueberry scone, consider this: High fructose corn syrup, despite all the media hype, is nutritionally the same as the table sugar that people add to their coffee.

The Many Kinds of Sugar

"High fructose corn syrup is one of the most misunderstood products in the food supply," said Harvard's David Ludwig on NBC Nightly News recently. That's because sugar is sugar, whether it's made from beets, cane, or corn. They're nearly identical in molecular composition, and exactly equal in sweetness and calorie content.

Yet crafty marketers have been perpetuating the myth that some sweeteners are healthier than others. How do they pull it off?

In part by confusing pure fructose with high fructose corn syrup. Table sugar is made of a half-and-half recipe of fructose and glucose. High fructose corn syrup, on the other hand, contains either 42 or 55 percent fructose. The rest, as with table sugar, is plain old glucose. So despite having "high fructose" in its name, HFCS has roughly the same amount of fructose as table sugar.

But with all the scientific names, it's easy for consumers to get confused. A study in April [2009] from the University of California–

FAST FACT

In the last few years, food companies such as the Sara Lee Corporation, ConAgra Foods, and PepsiCo have removed high fructose corn syrup from their products.

Davis, for example, demonized fructose as unsafe to consume in large (read: abnormal) quantities.

Putting aside the fact that consuming anything in absurd quantities is likely to have some bad effects, this fructose study didn't even deal with HFCS. It focused on pure fructose, which we don't find in the human diet anyway. As biochemist Dr. John S. White concluded, the UC–Davis study "did not test high-fructose corn syrup . . . and judgments should not be made about it from the findings."

High fructose corn syrup made from corn has roughly the same amount of fructose as cane sugar.

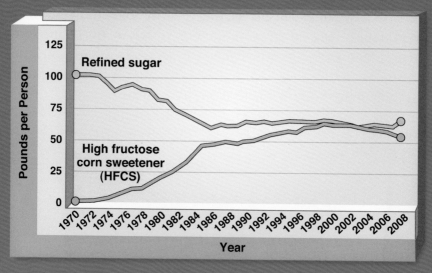

HFCS and Sugar Consumption, 1970–2008

Taken from: USDA Economic Research Service, "U.S. per Capita Food Availability: Sweeteners by Individual Caloric Sweetener," 2008. www.ers.usda.gov/.

The Evidence That HFCS Is Safe

The reality is this: The Food and Drug Administration puts HFCS in the category of ingredients that are "generally recognized as safe."

The agency also classifies HFCS as "natural."

A study in the *American Journal of Clinical Nutrition* shows that HFCS affects the body no differently than a wholesome glass of milk. And this past summer, the American Medical Association issued a report stating that "it appears unlikely that HFCS contributes more to obesity or other conditions than sucrose [table sugar]."

That's because these sweeteners are all nutritionally equivalent. Your body can hardly tell them apart.

Another set of five research papers in the *American Journal of Clinical Nutrition* confirmed that the No-HFCS doctrine is groundless. As *USA Today* reported, the studies found "no special link between consumption of high-fructose corn syrup and obesity." As one researcher put it, "sucrose and high-fructose corn syrup are not that different."

A Fad Diet Myth

Leading nutrition experts at the American Dietetic Association [ADA] denounce the "good" food, "bad" food campaigns backed by pseudoscience. (The ADA recommends that we focus on the amount, rather than the type of foods consumed.) Consuming HFCS, sugar, or other sweeteners in moderation is the key to a healthy diet.

Smart marketing doesn't change the facts. You won't be any healthier switching from high fructose corn syrup to table sugar—no matter what kind of sweet nothings your local barista whispers in your ear.

Instead of promoting a "Real Food" marketing gimmick, Starbucks executives might try reading some of the real science. If they keep basing culinary decisions on fad diet myths, the carbs in their bagels could disappear next. To say nothing of the caffeine in all that java.

EVALUATING THE AUTHOR'S ARGUMENTS:

In this viewpoint J. Justin Wilson says Starbucks's switch from high fructose corn syrup to sugar in their baked goods was pointless, since the two are essentially the same. Do you think that Jennifer Kelly, the author of the previous viewpoint, would approve of the switch made by Starbucks? Why or why not?

There Is No Evidence That Organic Food Is Safer than Conventional Food

Stephen Barrett

"Most studies conducted since the early 1970s have found that the pesticide levels in foods designated organic were similar to those that were not."

In the following viewpoint, Stephen Barrett claims that organic food is not better than conventional food. He claims that according to the USDA proposal, "No distinctions should be made between organically and non-organically produced products in terms of quality, appearance, or safety." Many studies have found that pesticide levels in organic and nonorganic foods are similar, and that the amount present is not enough to do much harm. Ultimately, Barrett concludes that the USDA Organic stamp will not protect a consumer or provide them with safer food. Stephen Barrett is a retired psychiatrist, author, and webmaster of Quackwatch.com.

The organic rules are intended to address production methods rather than the physical qualities of the products themselves. In a news release that accompanied the 1997 rules, [it] stated:

What is organic? Generally, it is agriculture produced through a natural as opposed to synthetic process. The natural portion of the definition is fairly obvious, but process is an equally critical distinction. When we certify organic, we are certifying not just a product but the farming and handling practices that yield it. When you buy a certified organic tomato, for instance, you are buying the product of an organic farm. And, consumers are willing to fork over a little more for that tomato. They've shown that they will pay a premium for organic food. National standards are our way of ensuring that consumers get what they pay for.

I disagree. Many consumers who "fork over a little more" believe that the foods themselves are more nutritious, safer, and tastier. But the USDA proposal itself noted that, "No distinctions should be made between organically and non-organically produced products in terms of quality, appearance, or safety." In other words, no claim should be made that the foods themselves are better—or even different! Some consumers believe that buying "organic" fosters agricultural practices that are better for the environment. . . .

More Nutritious?
Organic foods are certainly not more nutritious. The nutrient content of plants is determined primarily by heredity. Mineral content may be affected by the mineral content of the soil, but this has no significance

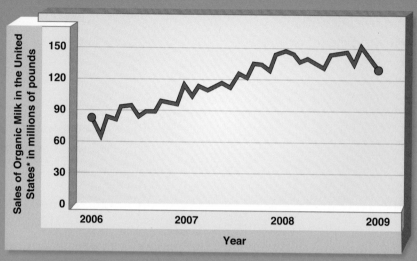

Decline in Demand for Organic Milk

After years of growth, demand is falling off.

*Does not include nonfluid products, like cheese, made with organic milk.

Taken from: Katie Zezima, "Organic Dairies Watch the Good Times Turn Bad," *New York Times*, May 28, 2009.
Original Source: Department of Agriculture.

in the overall diet. If essential nutrients are missing from the soil, the plant will not grow. If plants grow, that means the essential nutrients are present. Experiments conducted for many years have found no difference in the nutrient content of organically grown crops and those grown under standard agricultural conditions.

Safer?

Many "organic" proponents suggest that their foods are safer because they have lower levels of pesticide residues. However, the pesticide levels in our food supply are not high. In some situations, pesticides even reduce health risks by preventing the growth of harmful organisms, including molds that produce toxic substances.

To protect consumers, the FDA sets tolerance levels in foods and conducts frequent "market basket" studies wherein foods from regions throughout the United States are purchased and analyzed. Its 1997 tests found that about 60% of fruits and vegetables had no detectable pesticides and only about 1.2% of domestic and 1.6% of imported foods had violative levels. Its annual Total Diet Study has always found that America's dietary intakes are well within international and Environmental Protection Agency standards.

Most studies conducted since the early 1970s have found that the pesticide levels in foods designated organic were similar to those that were not. In 1997, *Consumer Reports* purchased about a thousand pounds of tomatoes, peaches, green bell peppers, and apples in five cities and tested them for more than 300 synthetic pesticides. Traces were detected in 77% of conventional foods and 25% of organically labeled foods, but only one sample of each exceeded the federal limit.

Pesticides can locate on the surface of foods as well as beneath the surface. The amounts that washing can remove depends on their location, the amount and temperature of the rinse water, and whether detergent is used. Most people rinse their fruits and vegetables with plain water before eating them. In fact, *Consumer Reports on Health* has recommended this. *Consumer Reports* stated that it did not do so because the FDA tests unwashed products. The amount of pesticide removed by simple rinsing has not been scientifically studied but is probably small. *Consumer Reports* missed a golden opportunity to assess this.

Do pesticides found in conventional foods pose a health threat? Does the difference in pesticide content warrant buying "organic" foods? *Consumer Reports* equivocates: "For consumers in general, the unsettling truth is that no one really knows what a lifetime of consuming the tiny quantities of [pesticides on] foods might do to a person. The effect, if any, is likely to be small for most individuals—but may be significant for the population at large." But the editors also advise, "No one should avoid fruits and vegetables for fear of pesticides; the health benefits of these foods overwhelm any possible risk."

Manfred Kroger, Ph.D., Quackwatch consultant and Professor of Food Science at The Pennsylvania State University, has put the matter more bluntly:

Scientific agriculture has provided Americans with the safest and most abundant food supply in the world. Agricultural chemicals are needed to maintain this supply. The risk from pesticide residue, if any, is minuscule, is not worth worrying about, and does not warrant paying higher prices. . . .

Better for the Environment?

Many buyers of "organic" foods believe that the extra money they pay will ultimately benefit the environment by encouraging more farmers to use "organic" methods. But doing this cannot have much effect because "organic" agriculture is too inefficient to meet the world's food needs. Moreover, the dividing line between organic and conventional agriculture is not sharp because various practices are not restricted to one or the other. For example, "organic" farmers tend not to use pesticides, but faced with threatened loss of crops, they may change their mind. If certain patterns of pesticide use cause more harm than good and there is a way to remedy the situation, the people concerned about it can seek regulatory solutions. I don't believe that paying extra for food will benefit anybody but those who sell it. . . .

The Bottom Line

The revised rules went into effect on October 21, 2002. The latest USDA definition states:

> Organic food is produced by farmers who emphasize the use of renewable resources and the conservation of soil and water to enhance environmental quality for future generations. Organic meat, poultry, eggs, and dairy products come from animals that are given no antibiotics or growth hormones. Organic food is produced without using most conventional pesticides; petroleum-based fertilizers or sewage sludge–based fertilizers; bio-engineering; or ionizing radiation. Before a product can be labeled "organic," a Government-approved certifier inspects the farm where the food is grown to make sure the farmer is following all the rules necessary to meet USDA organic standards. Companies that handle or process organic food before it gets to your local supermarket or restaurant must be certified, too.

Organic farms use different methods of production than those of conventional farms. Organic farms do not give hormone supplements or administer antibiotics to their cows.

A comprehensive review published the same year concluded:

- Studies comparing foods derived from organic and conventional growing systems were assessed for three key areas: nutritional value, sensory quality, and food safety. It is evident from this assessment that there are few well-controlled studies that are capable of making a valid comparison. With the possible exception of nitrate content, there is no strong evidence that organic and conventional foods differ in concentrations of various nutrients.
- While there are reports indicating that organic and conventional fruits and vegetables may differ on a variety of sensory qualities, the findings are inconsistent.
- While it is likely that organically grown foods are lower in pesticide residues, there has been very little documentation of residue levels.

In 2006, the Institute of Food Technologists concluded:

While many studies demonstrate . . . qualitative differences between organic and conventional foods, it is premature to conclude that either food system is superior to the other with respect to safety or nutritional composition. Pesticide residues, naturally occurring toxins, nitrates, and polyphenolic compounds exert their health risks or benefits on a dose-related basis, and data do not yet exist to ascertain whether the differences in the levels of such chemicals between organic foods and conventional foods are of biological significance.

Nevertheless, if you want to pay extra for your food, the U.S. Government will help you do so. Violators of the rules can be fined up to $10,000 per violation. But organic "certification," no matter what the rules, will not protect consumers. Foods certified as "organic" will neither be safer nor more nutritious than "regular" foods. Nor is there any logical reason to conclude that they have any special disease-curing properties. They will just cost more and may lessen public confidence in the safety of "ordinary" foods. Instead of legitimizing health nonsense, our government should do more to attack its spread.

EVALUATING THE AUTHOR'S ARGUMENTS:

In this viewpoint, Stephen Barrett argues for regular food over organic food. Does Barrett address the main concern of Peter Melchett, author of the following viewpoint? Explain.

There Is No Evidence That Pesticides Are Safe in Foods

Peter Melchett

"It seems that some man-made chemicals may have a significant impact on our health in very small doses, measured in parts per billion or parts per trillion."

In the following viewpoint Peter Melchett argues that the public concern about pesticides in food should be taken seriously. Melchett claims that there is no way to prove with absolute certainty that pesticides are safe. In addition, he sees a few fundamental problems with pesticides: He says that just because pesticides may increase food yield does not mean they are good. Second, he says pesticides affect some people more than others, making it difficult to base safety on an average. Third, he worries that the results of consuming a combination of pesticides have not been studied, which is related to the fourth problem that data about pesticides is secret. Finally, he says that modern toxicology is finding that very minute levels of chemicals can have profound effects. He concludes that the safety regulation of pesticides needs to include the option to stop their use. Melchett is policy director of the Soil Association, an organic food and farming organization in the United Kingdom.

1. According to Melchett, at what point in history were pesticides introduced?
2. What are the three possible effects of eating pesticides in combination, according to the author?
3. Decisions about the use of pesticides need to be informed by what other than science, according to Melchett?

I t is pretty obvious that pesticides kill things. That is what they are designed to do. Weedkillers kill plants, insecticides kill insects, and fungicides kill fungal spores and often (unexpectedly) a lot of insects as well. Apart from chemical weapons, these are the only substances we deliberately release into the environment in order to kill things.

So it seems a bit silly for the *Guardian*'s letter and comment pages to have been busy over the last couple of weeks [during March to April 2006] with serious assessments about whether pesticides are "dangerous" or "safe." They are clearly designed to be dangerous.

A Legitimate Concern

There is great public unease about pesticides in food. A new EU [European Union]-funded study has just confirmed that pesticides in food are the number one food safety concern for citizens in the EU (they questioned 24,642 people in the EU, including 1,334 in the UK [United Kingdom]). The reaction to this real (and I think fully justified) unease has been to over-claim the safety of pesticides in food. The claim that they are safe comes not only from the pesticide industry, but from almost all scientists on the government's regulatory bodies that assess pesticide safety, the National Farmers Union and almost all the Department for Environment, Food and Rural Affairs. In reality, the scientific evidence could only justify a claim that pesticides are "as safe as we can make them while allowing their continued, widespread use."

But they fear this will not "reassure" consumers, so they over-claim. For example, in the *Guardian* this week [in April 2006], Dr Chris Tyler says "there is no discernible risk to consumers." Dr Ian Brown, chairman of the government's pesticide residues committee, claimed that the pesticides that his committee finds in the food that we eat "will not affect our health." Realising that such an absolute statement can never be justified by the scientific evidence, which will always be tentative in an area like this, Dr Brown modified his position to say that the pesticides in food provided to school children give "no grounds for concern."

What you and I decide to get concerned about is really no business of Dr Brown's, and certainly something that he and his committee have little expertise in. He was looking for a way of expressing his total conviction that the system he oversees delivers safe food, while trying not to make the same mistake that government scientists made before mad cow disease. Then false statements that beef was "safe" to eat rightly caused lasting damage to public confidence in claims by government and industry scientists.

A Biased System

So the public are concerned, and scientists, chemical companies and some farmers want to claim absolute safety, but in reality, they cannot. However, supporters of pesticides face a number of other even more fundamental problems.

First, these chemicals were introduced in a post second world war era when not only was food in short supply, but scientists, and anything

Organic Food Seen as Safer for Environment

"Do you think the following statements are true or false for organic foods?"

	True (%)	False (%)
It is more expensive	95	5
It is grown without pesticides	84	16
It is safer for the environment	79	21
It is healthier	76	24
It tastes better	39	61

Taken from: Harris poll #97, October 8, 2007.

"scientific" or "technical" was considered to have near miraculous and certainly unchallengeable benefits for society as a whole. In those days, men in white coats could do no wrong. Five or six decades later, the advocates of pesticides are still working in a system designed to make pesticide use possible with the minimum of fuss and public scrutiny, and with safety, promotion and authorisation all covered by the same government department.

The regulatory committees are generally one-dimensional, made up of scientists who have the same world view, and who tend to agree with each other. While this is very slowly changing, it is hard for those involved to look other than biased because the system they operate is biased. This situation has drawn criticism from the royal commission on environmental pollution in an excellent recent report, unusual for the strength of criticism of an official system still staunchly defended by fellow scientists involved in it.

A Lack of Safety Assessments

Second, we now know that some groups of people—the unborn foetus [fetus], young children and the elderly—are likely to be much more susceptible to the effect of pesticides in their food than the rest of us. Worse (for the pesticide industry and regulators, and not least for

One of the problems of assessing the effects of pesticides on humans is that pesticide manufacturers' assessments are based on industry-selected, confidential data that has not been peer reviewed.

the people concerned), it seems that some individuals may be especially susceptible, and particularly at risk. If we want all groups, and all individuals, to be "safe" (or, more realistically, as safe as possible), pesticides should be regulated in a way that protects the most vulnerable. In fact, in general, safety limits in the UK are set by reference to the average (a few other countries do add additional safety factors to protect the very young).

Third, it is physically impossible to test pesticides in a way that reflects the reality of how we actually eat them—in a combination of foods, any of which may contain a mixture of pesticides (the "cocktail" effect). Eating pesticides in combination may mean they cancel each other out, they may have an additive impact, or they may react synergistically, multiplying their respective impacts. We really do not know. Nor is there any way that the millions upon millions of theoretical mixtures and doses could be tested, even looking at pesticides alone, and ignoring all the other sources of similar chemicals that we get in our bodies from air pollution, household cleaners, fire-retardants in furniture, gardening and so on.

Fourth, in order to protect companies' interest in making a profit out of new chemicals, all pesticide safety assessments are based on industry-selected and usually confidential data, and generally not on peer-reviewed published science. If any scientist is asked what makes something "scientific," they are bound to include the system of peer review, followed by the disclosure through publishing the details of experiments and data on which conclusions are based. It is this that allows replication, another key defining element of "science." But, although the committees who do this work are usually called "scientific" committees, and they are made up of scientists, they actually base their decisions on information that does not reach the accepted standard of "science."

Modern Toxicology

Fifth, the whole of the government's safety testing apparatus (and indeed traditional toxicology) rests on the idea that if you reduce pesticides in food to small enough quantities they will have no discernible effect on living organisms, including us. The (not unreasonable) theory is that you eventually get such a small dose of pesticides in your food that it doesn't have any discernible effect at all. Also, again not unreasonably, scientists assumed that the adverse effect that a pesticide has on people will increase the more of it they eat, and decrease the less they eat (until you reach that no discernible effect point).

Modern toxicology is challenging both assumptions, and this has been set out authoritatively by Professor Vyvyan Howard, one of a small minority on the government's advisory committee on pesticides expressing dissent from the conventional view. It seems that some man-made chemicals may have a significant impact on our health in very small doses, measured in parts per billion or parts per trillion. Safety testing of pesticides, and the checking to see what is in our food, generally works in higher doses, of parts per million. It is also now being suggested that some new chemicals may have a damaging impact in small doses, that the impact then reduces for a while as the amount of pesticide consumed increases, and then after a certain point, dose and impact both increase together.

This is science. Challenging old assumptions, working at levels of sophistication not possible in past decades, challenging widely held assumptions, and putting forward new theories to be tested by others. And it is being rubbished by an organisation that has the unmitigated cheek to call itself Sense about Science, the organisation Dr Chris Tyler works for.

The Balance of Risk and Benefit

Safety regulation involves a series of political decisions being made about balances of risk and benefit. These decisions will be informed by science, but also by an assessment of need (are we starving, how desperate are we for food at a possible long term cost to our health). These decisions include whether to consider available alternatives that don't involve the use of pesticides (such as the growing organic market); whether or not we want to encourage pesticide-based farming because of the economic benefits it brings pesticide companies, or other significant economic interests and so on. All these political decisions about pesticide safety have been taken in ways that allow or encourage the use of pesticides—but even their existence is generally denied by the scientists involved.

Obviously, as an organic farmer, and someone working for the Soil Association (the main organic organisation in the UK), I have a vested interest in people accepting that farming with pesticides, and food containing pesticides, is as dangerous as I think it is. I started organic farming because of the terrible declines in wildlife, especially farmland birds, on our farm, which I experienced for myself in the decades from the mid 50s. These declines were not just caused by pesticides, but also by changes in cropping patterns and other factors (most in turn made possible by the use of pesticides), but they played the major part. Since going organic, the wildlife has returned.

I know that birds that live their whole lives in fields that are sprayed with pesticides will be more affected, or affected sooner, than people (who don't live in fields). But I am sure that what is good for skylarks and English partridges is also good for us.

EVALUATING THE AUTHOR'S ARGUMENTS:

In this viewpoint Peter Melchett contends that a claim that pesticides do not affect human health could never be justified and will always be tentative. If this is true, what other information should be used in determining whether or not to use pesticides?

Facts About Food Safety

Food Safety Regulation

US government agencies with food safety oversight:

- US Department of Agriculture: The Food Safety and Inspection Service of the Agriculture Department works to ensure that the commercial supply of meat, poultry, and egg products is safe, wholesome, and properly labeled and packaged.
- US Food and Drug Administration (FDA): This agency is responsible for regulation of food safety for all foods except meat, poultry, and egg products.

Food-Borne Illness

According to the Centers for Disease Control and Prevention:

- Each year roughly 1 out of 6 Americans (or 48 million people) get sick, 128,000 are hospitalized, and 3,000 die of food-borne diseases.
- The top five pathogens contributing to domestically acquired food-borne illnesses are: norovirus, salmonella, clostridium, campylobacter, and staphylococcus.
- Of the top five pathogens, the top pathogen resulting in hospitalization is salmonella.
- Salmonella is the number one cause of death, causing over a quarter of all food-borne illness fatalities each year.
- Poultry (chicken, turkey, and duck) was found to be the top cause of food-borne illness from 2003 to 2008.

Genetically Modified, or Bioengineered, Foods

- The three top genetically modified crops in the United States are cotton, soybeans, and corn; 93 percent of soybeans and 86 percent of corn is genetically modified.
- The US Food and Drug Administration does not require labeling of bioengineered foods.
- The US Food and Drug Administration has not approved any genetically engineered animals for human consumption, though applications for such are under consideration.

- Several countries have banned the cultivation of genetically modified food, including Austria, France, Germany, Greece, Hungary, and Luxembourg.

Food Irradiation
- In 1963 the US Food and Drug Administration determined the irradiation of food to be safe.
- Food irradiation is a process in which approved foods are exposed to radiant energy, including gamma rays, electron beams, and X-rays.
- According to the Food Safety and Inspection Service, irradiation of food reduces harmful bacteria, including E. coli, salmonella, and campylobacter.
- In the United States the following foods are approved for irradiation: meat and poultry, wheat, white potatoes, many spices, dry vegetable seasonings, fresh shell eggs, and fresh produce.
- The US Food and Drug Administration requires that irradiated food bear a special symbol—the Radura—with the statement "treated with radiation" or "treated by irradiation," although consideration of eliminating the labeling requirement is under way.

Public Opinion About Food Safety
According to a 2008 Consumer Reports National Research Center poll:
- Twelve percent rate the nation's food supply as very safe, 61 percent as somewhat safe, 21 percent as somewhat unsafe, and 5 percent as very unsafe.
- Fifty-four percent agree that the government is doing all it can to ensure the safety of America's food supply, whereas 45 percent disagree.
- Eighty-one percent are concerned about the safety of imported foods.
- Sixty-nine percent believe that the FDA should inspect foreign food-processing facilities at least once a month.
- Ninety-five percent agree that food products made from genetically engineered animals should be labeled as such.
- Twenty-nine percent would buy meat or milk products from genetically engineered animals if they were available.

- Ninety-two percent agree that irradiated meat should be labeled as such.
- Forty-nine percent would pay more for meat products labeled as tested for mad cow disease.
- Fifty-seven percent would pay more for dairy products produced without artificial growth hormones.
- Sixty-nine percent agree that cloning of food animals should be prohibited.

Organizations to Contact

The editors have compiled the following list of organizations concerned with the issues debated in this book. The descriptions are derived from materials provided by the organizations. All have publications or information available for interested readers. The list was compiled on the date of publication of the present volume; the information provided here may change. Be aware that many organizations take several weeks or longer to respond to inquiries, so allow as much time as possible for the receipt of requested materials.

American Council on Science and Health (ACSH)
1995 Broadway, 2nd Fl., New York, NY 10023-5860
(212) 362-7044
fax: (212) 362-4919
e-mail: acsh@acsh.org
website: www.acsh.org

The ACSH is a consumer education group concerned with issues related to food, nutrition, chemicals, pharmaceuticals, lifestyle, the environment, and health. The ACSH works to add reason and balance to debates about public health issues such as food safety. It publishes the quarterly newsletter *Priorities* and publications about chemicals in food.

American Farm Bureau Federation (AFBF)
600 Maryland Ave. SW, Ste. 1000W, Washington, DC 20024
(202) 406-3600 • fax: (202) 406-3602
e-mail: webmaster@fb.org
website: www.fb.org

The AFBF is an independent organization governed by and representing farm and ranch families, with the goal of enhancing and strengthening the lives of rural Americans and building strong, prosperous agricultural communities. The AFBF works as a grassroots organization at all levels to analyze problems and formulate action to achieve educational improvement, economic opportunity, and social advancement, and to promote the national well-being. The AFBF has a variety of publications on legislation affecting food safety, including *Food Safety and Labeling*.

Center for Consumer Freedom
PO Box 34557, Washington, DC 20043
(202) 463-7112
website: www.consumerfreedom.com

The Center for Consumer Freedom is a nonprofit organization devoted to promoting personal responsibility and protecting consumer choices. The Center for Consumer Freedom uses ad campaigns and newspaper op-eds to combat measures that attempt to restrict consumer freedom to eat and drink what one wants. These ad campaigns and op-eds, as well as games and cartoons, are available at its website.

Center for Food Safety (CFS)
660 Pennsylvania Ave. SE, #302, Washington DC 20003
(202) 547-9359 • fax: (202) 547-9429
e-mail: office@centerforfoodsafety.org
website: www.centerforfoodsafety.org

The CFS is a nonprofit public interest organization established for the purpose of challenging harmful food production technologies and promoting sustainable alternatives. The CFS combines multiple tools and strategies in pursuing its goals, including litigation and legal petitions for rule making, legal support for various sustainable agriculture and food safety constituencies, as well as public education, grassroots organizing, and media outreach. The CFS publishes reports available at its website, including *Food Irradiation: A Gross Failure*.

Center for Global Food Issues (CGFI)
PO Box 202, Churchville, VA 24421
(540) 337-6354
fax: (540) 337-8593
website: www.cgfi.org

The CGFI, a project of the Hudson Institute, works to promote free trade, combat efforts to limit technological innovation in agriculture, and heighten awareness of the connection between agricultural productivity and environmental conservation. The CGFI uses its worldwide overview of food and farming to assess policies, improve farmers' understanding of the new globalized farm economy, and heighten awareness of the environmental impacts of various farming systems and food policies. Available at the CGFI's website are videos of speeches by CGFI staff and CGFI reports.

Center for Science in the Public Interest (CSPI)
1875 Connecticut Ave. NW, Ste. 300, Washington, DC 20009
(202) 332-9110
e-mail: cspi@cspinet.org
website: www.cspinet.org

The CSPI is an organization advocating for nutrition and health, food safety, alcohol policy, and sound science. The CSPI is currently working to get junk foods out of school, eliminate trans fats from the food supply, reduce sodium in foods, and improve food safety laws. The CSPI publishes the newsletter *Nutrition Action Healthletter* and has over a decade of newsletters available at its website.

Food & Water Watch
1616 P St. NW, Ste. 300, Washington, DC 20036
(202) 683-2500
fax: (202) 683-2501
e-mail: info@fwwatch.org
website: www.foodandwaterwatch.org

Food & Water Watch works to ensure the food, water, and fish we consume are safe, accessible, and sustainably produced. Food & Water Watch promotes policies that lead to sustainable, healthy food; advocates for safe and affordable drinking water; and promotes policies that maintain the environmental quality of the ocean. Food & Water Watch publishes fact sheets and reports, such as *The Poisoned Fruit of American Trade Policy.*

Food Safety and Inspection Service (FSIS)
1400 Independence Ave. SW, Washington, DC 20250-3700
(202) 720-3781
fax: (202) 720-6050
e-mail: fsis.outreach@usda.gov
website: www.fsis.usda.gov

The FSIS is the public health agency in the US Department of Agriculture responsible for ensuring the safety of the nation's commercial supply of meat, poultry, and egg products. The FSIS enforces food regulations and policies and gives information about recalls and public health alerts. Available at its website is information about recalls, regulations, and Ask Karen, a food safety knowledge base.

Institute for Responsible Technology
PO Box 469, Fairfield, IA 52556
(641) 209-1765
e-mail: info@responsibletechnology.org
website: www.responsibletechnology.org

The Institute for Responsible Technology is an organization working to educate policy makers and the public about genetically modified organisms (GMOs). The Institute for Responsible Technology investigates and reports on the risks of GMOs and their impact on health, environment, the economy, and agriculture, as well as the problems associated with current research, regulation, corporate practices, and reporting. The Institute for Responsible Technology has several brochures available at its website.

Organic Consumers Association (OCA)
6771 S. Silver Hill Dr., Finland, MN 55603
(218) 226-4164
fax: (218) 353-7652
website: www.organicconsumers.org

The OCA is a nonprofit public interest organization campaigning for health, justice, and sustainability. The OCA focuses on promoting the views and interests of the nation's estimated 50 million organic and socially responsible consumers. The OCA publishes a weekly e-mail newsletter, *Organic Bytes.*

Union of Concerned Scientists (UCS)
2 Brattle Sq., Cambridge, MA 02138-3780
(617) 547-5552
fax: (617) 864-9405
website: www.ucsusa.org

The UCS is a science-based nonprofit organization working for a healthy environment and a safer world. The UCS combines independent scientific research and citizen action to develop innovative, practical solutions and to secure responsible changes in government policy, corporate practices, and consumer choices. The UCS publishes the monthly *FEED—Food and Environment Electronic Digest.*

For Further Reading

Books

Cummings, Claire Hope. *Uncertain Peril: Genetic Engineering and the Future of Seeds.* Boston: Beacon, 2008. Expresses concern that the rise of industrial agriculture and plant biotechnology, the fall of public interest science, and the patenting of seeds is threatening our survival.

Fortin, Neal D. *Food Regulation: Law, Science, Policy, and Practice.* Hoboken, NJ: Wiley, 2009. Discusses the federal statutes, regulations, and regulatory agencies involved in food regulation.

Imhoff, Daniel. *Foodfight: The Citizen's Guide to a Food and Farm Bill.* Healdsburg, CA: Watershed Media, 2007. Offers an overview of the federal Farm Bill, including its impacts on the country's rural economies, health and nutrition, and biodiversity.

Miller, Henry I., and Gregory Conko. *The Frankenfood Myth: How Protest and Politics Threaten the Biotech Revolution.* Westport, CT: Praeger, 2004. Traces the origins of the backlash against food biotechnology, claiming that a conspiracy against technology has resulted in unnecessary regulation.

Morrone, Michele. *Poisons on Our Plates: The Real Food Safety Problem in the United States.* Westport, CT: Praeger, 2008. Explores the impact of bacteria and viruses on the food supply and how they can make people sick, advocating changes to the nation's environmental health policies.

Nestle, Marion. *Safe Food: The Politics of Food Safety.* Berkeley and Los Angeles: University of California Press, 2010. Argues that ensuring safe food involves not only washing hands and cooking food to higher temperatures, but also politics.

Paarlberg, Robert. *Food Politics: What Everyone Needs to Know.* New York: Oxford University Press, 2010. Examines issues on today's global food landscape, including farming, obesity, food safety, organic food, and genetically engineered food.

Park, Moby, and Miyun Park, eds. *Gristle: From Factory Farms to Food Safety*. New York: New Press, 2010. Fifteen authors from a variety of backgrounds argue that industrial animal agriculture unnecessarily harms workers, communities, the environment, people's health and finances, and animals.

Pollan, Michael. *In Defense of Food: An Eater's Manifesto*. New York: Penguin, 2008. Claims that real food is disappearing and proposes that what we eat be informed by ecology and tradition, not just science.

Richardson, Jill. *Recipe for America: Why Our Food System Is Broken and What We Can Do to Fix It*. Brooklyn: Ig, 2009. Argues that sustainable agriculture—where local farms raise food that is healthy and does not damage the environment—offers the only solution to America's food crisis.

Rodale, Maria. *Organic Manifesto: How Organic Food Can Heal Our Planet, Feed the World, and Keep Us Safe*. New York: Rodale, 2010. Examines the alliances that have formed between the chemical companies that produce genetically altered seeds, the agricultural educational system, and the government, arguing for organic farming.

Smith, Jeffrey M. *Genetic Roulette: The Documented Health Risks of Genetically Engineered Foods*. Fairfield, IA: Yes!, 2007. Argues against the biotechnology industry's claim that genetically modified foods are safe.

Specter, Michael. *Denialism: How Irrational Thinking Hinders Scientific Progress, Harms the Planet, and Threatens Our Lives*. New York: Penguin, 2009. Charges that the disdain for technologies such as genetically modified organisms shows that there is a war against scientific progress.

Periodicals and Internet Sources

Bergen County (NJ) Record. "Keep Our Food Safe: FDA Isn't Doing Its Job Well Enough," February 5, 2009.

Bidstrup, Jeff. "Who Benefits from GM Crops?," *Truth About Trade and Technology*, February 19, 2009. www.truthabouttrade.org.

Boston Globe. "State Shouldn't Be Cowed by Raw-Milk Aficionados," May 22, 2010.

Canter, Laura. "Shattering Myths Behind Frankenfoods: The Benefits Behind Genetically Engineered Produce," *Food and Drink Digital*, September 26, 2010. www.foodanddrinkdigital.com.

Cendrowicz, Leo. "Is Europe Finally Ready for Genetically Modified Foods?," *Time*, March 9, 2010.

Christian Science Monitor. "Frankenfish—Genetically Modified Salmon—Take Food and Ecology to a New Level," September 22, 2010.

Cohen, Adam. "100 Years Later, the Food Industry Is Still 'The Jungle,'" *New York Times*, January 2, 2007.

Cook, Christopher D. "Put Some More Meat into US Food Safety Rules," *Madison (WI) Capital Times*, March 4, 2008.

Cummins, Ronnie. "10 Freakiest Things About Frankenfish," *Huffington Post*, September 23, 2010. www.huffingtonpost.com.

Falkenstein, Drew. "Raw Milk: An Issue of Safety or Freedom?," *Food Safety News*, April 19, 2010.

Food & Water Watch. "'Enviropig' or Frankenswine? Why Genetically Modifying Pigs Could Cause a Load of Manure," June 2010. www .foodandwaterwatch.org.

Giles-Smith, Karen. "Got (Pasteurized) Milk?," *Healthy & Fit*, October 2010.

Goodman, Jim. "Common Sense Could Go a Long Way to Promote Food Safety," *Madison (WI) Capital Times*, October 11, 2009.

Gumpert, David. "Getting Past 'Religion' in the Raw Milk War," *Food Safety News*, December 30, 2009.

Hansen, Michael. "Stop the Madness," *New York Times*, June 20, 2008.

Henderson, Mark. "Organic Farmers Must Embrace GM Crops If We Are to Feed the World, Says Scientist," *Times* (London), January 13, 2010.

Institute for Responsible Technology. "State-of-the-Science on the Health Risks of GM Foods," February 15, 2010. www.responsibletechnology.net.

Joy, Nick. "Why Genetically Modified Salmon Affects My Rights as a Citizen," *Huffington Post*, October 19, 2010. www.huffingtonpost.com.

Kleckner, Dean. "A Sustainable Solution," *Truth About Trade and Technology*, December 12, 2008. www.truthabouttrade.org.

Krome, Margaret. "Food Safety Bills Reach Too Far, Cost Too Much," *Madison (WI) Capital Times*, January 19, 2010.

Krugman, Paul. "Bad Cow Disease," *New York Times*, June 13, 2008.

Laskawy, Tom. "What a 'Sweet Surprise'! HFCS Contains More Fructose than Believed," *Grist*, October 26, 2010. www.grist.org.

Lettice, Eoin. "We Need GM Plants That Benefit Consumers and Not Just Farmers," *Guardian* (Manchester, UK), March 8, 2010.

Logomasini, Angela. "Seeking Food Safety, Getting Human Harm: Food-Borne Illness Could Result from BPA Ban," *Washington Times*, August 25, 2010.

Markheim, Daniella, and Caroline Walsh. "A Safe and Bountiful Harvest: How to Ensure America's Food Safety," *Backgrounder*, January 10, 2008. www.policyarchive.org.

Marler, Bill. "Long Past Time to Pass the Food Safety Bill," *Food Safety News*, October 4, 2010. www.foodsafetynews.com.

McCarthy, Jim. "Farmers Feed the World," *Truth About Trade and Technology*, October 30, 2009. www.truthabouttrade.org.

McWilliams, James. "The Evils of Corn Syrup: How Food Writers Got It Wrong," *Atlantic*, September 21, 2010.

Menon, Amarnath K. "GM Food: How Safe Is It?," *India Today*, November 2, 2009.

Miller, Henry. "The FDA Needs Egging On," *Guardian* (Manchester, UK), August 24, 2010.

Paarlberg, Robert. "Attention Whole Food Shoppers," *Foreign Policy*, May/June 2010.

Richardson, Jill. "The Battle over Raw Milk: Let's Ditch the Hysterics and Give People a Choice," *AlterNet*, October 29, 2009. www.alternet.org.

Roanoke (VA) Times. "Protect Food Safety: Poisoned Peanut Butter Should Prod Washington to Toughen Oversight of the Food Industry," February 8, 2009.

Roberts, Owen. "Cheap Food Is Not Safe Food," *Toronto Star*, September 15, 2008.

Schlosser, Eric. "Unsafe at Any Meal," *New York Times*, July 24, 2010.

Smith, Sylvia A. "Full Plate of Issues with World Food Supply," *Fort Wayne (IN) Journal Gazette*, March 21, 2010.

Stier, Jeff. "Soy Hypocritical," *Washington Times*, August 3, 2008.

Websites

Center for Foodborne Illness (www.foodborneillness.org). This website maintains a list of food-borne illnesses and food safety resources.

Foodsafety.gov (www.foodsafety.gov). This website contains information on food safety from a variety of US government agencies.

Safe Tables Our Priority (STOP) (www.safetables.org). This website contains information about food-borne illness, advocacy for food safety, and public policy resources.

Index

U

Union of Concerned Scientists, 52

University of California–Davis, 102–103

USA Today (newspaper), 104

USDA. *See* Department of Agriculture, US

USGS (US Geological Survey), 54

W

Washington Post (newspaper), 27

White, John S., 103

Wilson, J. Justin, 101

W.K. Kellogg Foundation, 24

World Organization for Animal Health (OIE), 95

Picture Credits